BEING PRESENT TO GOD

BEING PRESENT TO GOD

Letters on Prayer

by

HENRI CAFFAREL

Translated by Angeline Bouchard

Library of Congress Cataloging in Publication Data

Caffarel, Henri.
  Being Present to God.

  Translation of Présence à Dieu.
  1. Prayer. 2. Spiritual life—Catholic authors.
I. Title.
BV215.C3313   1983   248.3'2   83-15459
ISBN 0-8189-0462-3

Nihil Obstat:
Garrett Fitzgerald, S.J.
Censor Deputatus

Imprimatur:
✝ Joseph T. O'Keefe
Vicar General, Archbishop of New York
August 1, 1983

The Nihil Obstat and Imprimatur are
a declaration that a book or pamphlet is considered
to be free from doctrinal or moral error. It is not implied
that those who have granted the Nihil Obstat and
Imprimatur agree with the contents,
opinions or statements expressed.

Designed, printed and bound in the United States of
America by the Fathers and Brothers of the
Society of St. Paul, 2187 Victory Boulevard,
Staten Island, New York 10314, as part of their
communications apostolate.

1 2 3 4 5 6 7 8 9 (Current Printing: first digit)

Table of Contents

Introduction

Vatican II vigorously reminded the laity of the Gospel's demand that they be "present to the world." And yet—as has not always been sufficiently noted—it exhorted them with equal vigor to begin by becoming "present to God." Indeed, what would a "presence to the world" amount to by witnesses who have not been in close contact with the One about whom they are to witness, by spokesmen who do not listen to the One whose message they are to transmit, by laborers who do not follow the foreman's commands?

It is essentially during prayer that presence to God comes about. I am speaking of prayer that is first of all adoration and self-offering. That is why it has never been more urgent than now to initiate Christians into prayer and help them to pray, at a time when they are attaining a clearer awareness of their apostolic vocation and of their earthly tasks.

Such is the reason for this book of nearly a hundred letters on prayer. Most of them have already appeared in the *Cahiers sur l'oraison*. I have regrouped them into ten chapters, focusing on ten fundamental themes.

I beg the reader not to approach this book as if it were a treatise on prayer! If he did, he would be disappointed. These pages do not claim to say everything there is to say on the subject, and they were not written with the rigorous logic of a manual. They are a kind of directed exchange of views. In answer to a wide variety of spontaneous questions, they offer answers, using the familiar tone of conversation. The fact remains that a broad theology of prayer underlies these pages, as well as the experience of men and women of prayer, which has enriched Christian tradition over the centuries.

These texts should not be read one after the other in rapid succession. That would be to miss their message. The author's hope is that his readers will read no more than one letter a day, and that this letter be made the object of meditation and seen as an invitation to enter into God's intimate friendship.

There is no need to follow the order in which the letters are presented. It is for the reader to make his own selection as the need arises, with the help of the introductions that precede each chapter, presenting the theme of the letters in that chapter.

Above all, the reader should not read on when he feels drawn to interior silence. The Holy Spirit is the only true master of prayer. When he calls us from within, we must leave everything and listen attentively.

BEING PRESENT TO GOD

"The Teacher is here, asking for you" (Jn 11:28)

In defining friendship or love, we often limit ourselves to a description of the feelings and actions of one of the parties involved. This is an error to be found in many works dealing with mental prayer. They confine themselves to man's activity, whereas mental prayer is an encounter and a loving exchange between God and man.

When we go to mental prayer, we need to be convinced that we are expected, that God is there waiting for us.

1 *You are expected*—God is indeed everywhere. But it is at the heart of our being that he invites us to join him in the dialogue of love that is mental prayer.

2 *In the house of the Lord*—Let us learn how to express our feelings and thoughts spontaneously, simply to the One who is welcoming us.

3 *Speak to Him*—Our underlying attitudes are even more important than our words. And first among them is man's loving response to God's love, a response that consists in a stripping of self, in placing oneself totally at the Lord's service.

4 *The advice of the old parish priest*—There is authentic self-giving only when it is done here and now. There must be eager attention, a presence to God of our whole being, of all of our fully energized faculties.

5 *Being present to God*—But if our words and interior attitudes are to be pleasing to God, we must first ask him what he wants to tell us and what response he is expecting from us.

6 *"Speak, Lord, for your servant is listening"* (1 S 3:9)—Then, like any encounter of love, our mental prayer will be new and original each day, providing we bring to it an attentive and inventive heart.

7 *An invention of love*—For all our good intentions, our mental prayer often fails to come up to our expectations. It has not become a turning of all our faculties toward the Lord to be gathered into himself.

But by the very fact that our innermost self is turned toward God, our prayer is already genuine. It may even be quite advanced.

8 *The essential*—Do we need to make use of methods when mental prayer is difficult for us? In a certain sense, mental prayer is recalcitrant to methods, just like love. Be this as it may, certain laws govern dialogue. In our relations with God as well as with other humans, it is very important to know these laws.

9 *The practice of mental prayer*—But in the last analysis, the important thing is to bear in mind that prior to any initiative or industry on man's part, mental prayer is a gift from God.

10 *Mental prayer, a gift from God*

1. You are expected

We cannot help feeling forlorn when we arrive in a strange city (at the docks, the railroad or bus station, the airport) and know that nobody is there waiting for us. By contrast, if we are greeted by a cheerful face, if others reach out to help us, we have a wonderful sense of consolation. We are delivered from the cruel impression that somehow we have lost our way, that we are completely astray. The strangeness does not matter any more—the customs, the language, the vast disconcerting city. It is not so hard to be a stranger to everybody else, providing there is one person who thinks of us as a friend.

It is comforting, too, to discover that our hosts were expecting us. Our relatives and children don't need to say very much for us to sense it. Their attitude of welcome, the eagerness of their manner are enough. And when we are ushered to our room, we are finally convinced by the small vase of flowers, the book on art (because they know our tastes).

Dear friend, I wish that whenever you go to mental prayer you may always have the strong conviction of being expected: expected by the Father, the Son, and the Holy Spirit; expected within the Family of the Trinity. For your place is ready. Remember Christ's words: *"I am going to prepare a place for you"* (Jn 14:3). You may object that Jesus was speaking of heaven. True enough. But that is precisely what mental prayer is. It is heaven, at least in its essential reality: the presence of God, the love of God, God's welcome to his child.

The Lord is always expecting us. Better still, when we have barely made a few steps toward him, he comes out to meet us. Remember the parable: *"While he was still a long way off, his father caught sight of him and was deeply moved. He ran out to meet him, threw his arms around his neck, and kissed him"* (Lk 15:20). This son had grievously offended his father. He was expected nonetheless, impatiently expected.

2. In the house of the Lord

Stephen and Sylvia, a childless couple, both physicians, came to see me before leaving for the remote bushland where the two of them, alone except for the company of two missionaries, are to dedicate themselves to a completely new Christian community. They know it will be hard, and that in order to persevere they will need to pray a great deal. So they came to ask me to speak to them one last time about mental prayer, to give them essential advice on it. And as they left me, they insisted that I put into writing for them what I had just said.

My dear friends, for centuries the roads and bypaths of Judea witnessed, several times a year, unending streams of men, women, and children on their way to Jerusalem.

The slopes of the Judean mountains were steep, shade was rare, the sun beat down relentlessly, but nothing could discourage these devout Jews from going to the holy mountain.

The sentiments that guided them, that sustained their courage, are known to us. We find them echoed in the many Psalms they sang as they walked, their pilgrim hymns.

* * *

> *"How lovely is your dwelling place,*
> *O Lord of hosts!*
> *My soul yearns and pines*
> *for the courts of the Lord.*
> *My heart and my flesh*
> *cry out for the living God. . . .*
> *I had rather lie at the threshold of*
> *the house of my God*
> *than dwell in the tents of the wicked."* (Ps 84:2, 3, 11)
> *"I rejoiced because they said to me,*
> *'We will go up to the house of the Lord.'"* (Ps 122:1)

**

Once back home, when the hour of prayer arrived, wherever they were—in the house or in the fields—they turned towards Jerusalem to praise the Almighty.

There can be only one explanation for such a passionate love of their capital, such dedication to their Temple, such fidelity over the centuries. Jerusalem was much more than the capital of the kingdom. It was the City of the Lord, and the Temple was his house where they were always sure of finding him.

It was the desire to find God, to encounter him—the most basic aspiration of every religious person—that set in motion these throngs of believers, these seekers after God whose fervor is revealed in the Psalms.

Christ came. He manifested his love for Jerusalem, and his respect for the Father's House. At the same time, he declared that the Temple had lost its meaning, and would soon disappear. At the hour of his death on the Cross, the veil of the Holy of Holies was torn, as if indeed to signify that this temple was now desacralized. It would be replaced by a new, imperishable temple, "rebuilt in three days," the temple of his body, of his Mystical Body. There alone would men and women henceforth be able to find God.

But everyone who enters this temple becomes in their turn the dwelling place of God. Jesus has assured us of this: *"Anyone who loves me will be true to my word, and my Father will love him: we will come to him and make our dwelling place with him"* (Jn 14:23).

This is an astonishing revelation. Did God desert the Temple in order to come and dwell in the souls of his faithful? Yes. St. Paul says so explicitly: *"Are you not aware that you are the temple of God, and that the Spirit of God dwells in you?"* (1 Cor 3:16). *"You are the temple of the living God"* (2 Cor 6:16).

This word "temple" is not very meaningful for us. But under the pen of the Apostle trained from childhood to venerate and love the Temple of Jerusalem, it assumed its full meaning. In these texts the word translated by "temple" would be more aptly rendered by "holy of holies," the heart of the Temple, the locus of the divine presence.

And so God is within us, within the very heart of our being: present, living, loving and acting. It is there that he calls us. It is there that he is waiting for us, to unite us to himself.

God is there, but we're not. Our existence is spent outside ourselves, or at least on the periphery of our being, in the zone of sensations, emotions, imaginings, discussions; in that noisy and anxiety-ridden suburb of the soul. And if we happen to think of God, to yearn to encounter him, we go out of ourselves. We seek him on the outside, forgetting that he is right there within us.

We do not know the paths of our soul that will lead us into the subterranean and luminous chamber where God dwells. Or else, if we do know them, we lack the courage that impelled the fervent Jews to follow the roads to the Holy City. Is it a more arduous undertaking to reach the center of ourselves than it was for the Jews to go to Jerusalem?

Mental prayer means getting away from the tumultuous suburb of our being of which I just spoke. It is to recollect, to gather up all our faculties and plunge into the arid night that leads to the depths of our soul. Once on the threshold of the sanctuary, we need only to be silent and attentive. It is not a matter of spiritual sensation, of interior experience. It is a matter of *faith*: it means believing in the Presence. It means adoring the living Trinity in silence. It means offering and opening ourselves up to the overflowing life of the Triune God. It means cleaving to, and communing in, the eternal act of the Trinity.

Little by little, year by year, the core of our spiritual being will be refined by grace and become more sensible to the breathing of God, of the Spirit of love, within us. Little by little, we shall be divinized and our external life will become the manifestation, the epiphany of our interior life. We shall be holy because in our innermost being we shall be closely united to God All-Holy. We shall be fruitful, and rivers of living water will flow from us because we shall be joined to the very Wellspring of Life.

Dear friends, this is the "essential advice" that you ask of me. May it guide you safely to the hour of mental prayer in your remote bushland. I shall sum it up in a few words: to engage in mental prayer is to go on a pilgrimage to the sanctuary within, and there to adore the true God.

And if you want your whole life to become one long prayer, a life in God's presence, a life with God; if you want to become souls of prayer, you must, throughout the day, enter often within yourselves to adore the God who is expecting you there. It need not be for long. An instant's plunge inward, and then you can return to your tasks, your conversations; but you will return rejuvenated, refreshed, renewed.

In 17th-century France there lived a humble Carmelite lay brother, Lawrence of the Resurrection, who was well advanced in the spiritual life. He liked to tell those who came to him for advice, that there was no more effective way of attaining to a life of continual mental prayer, and hence a high degree of sanctity, than faithfulness to this practice. Hear his words: "During our work and our other activities, even when we are engaged in spiritual reading and writing, I say, even more—during our external devotions and vocal prayers—we must stop briefly, as often as we can, to adore God deep within our heart, to delight in him even if only in passing and as if by stealth."

> "O Lord, I love the house in which you dwell,
>   the tenting-place of your glory" (Ps 26:8).

When the Jews recited this Psalm, they thought of the Temple of Jerusalem. The Christian, for his part, thinks of his baptized soul.

3. Speak to Him

A few weeks ago, I visited a Trappist Monastery. The Guest-Master welcomed me, and led me to the Prior's office through the long, bright halls, redolent of poverty and silence. I entered a room with whitewashed walls, devoid of ornamentation and pictures, where a man of silence and serenity awaited me. His face was at once rugged and suffused with gentleness—a gentleness that did not speak to the senses but was completely spiritual, and that softened the sharp contours and hollows of his ascetical mask. In his glance, the candor of a child and the wisdom of old age mingled harmoniously. Our conversation took on a note of mutual trust. He was moved to speak of the day long ago which decided the course of his life.

As an adolescent he took part in the activities of a large Parisian church-related youth group. One Thursday during the winter, after a long afternoon of games, the curate talked about prayer to the older youths gathered in the small chapel. Our young man stayed on after his comrades, ostensibly to help the curate put things in order. Actually, he wanted to ask him something, but he scarcely knew how to go about it.

Finally, while sweeping the room—which was less embarrassing than in a tête-à-tête—he blurted out, "You're always telling us that we should pray, but you never teach us how to do it." The priest answered, "That's true! Do you want to know how to pray? Well, François, just go into the chapel and when you're there, speak to Him."

"That evening, I went to the chapel," the old monk continued. "I must have stayed a long time, because I remember getting home late and being severely reprimanded. For the first time in my life, I had prayed. And I do believe that, ever since, I have never stopped speaking to Him."

When he had finished making his disclosure, the Father Prior was silent. From a certain inflection in his voice, I understood that this memory from the distant past had had an emotional impact on him, for it was the first link in a long intimacy with his God. The silence continued. I did not dare break it. I was sure he was speaking to Him. Most certainly, he was thanking Him for leading him, when he was a lad of fifteen, to the priest who had directed his steps in the paths of prayer.

The curate's advice was only apparently banal. He was really proving that he was an experienced man of prayer who, rather than engage in a long discourse, was content to answer the teen-ager eager to learn to pray, with three words: "Speak to Him." We do not converse with shadows. In order to talk to God, we must become aware of his presence. And to know what to say to him, our faith must wake up and start searching. The need to formulate words prevents us from being satisfied with flimsy impressions. It forces us to express precise thoughts, intentions, sentiments. The merits of such a method are great, if one can really call this simple advice a method.

Many Christians, when they go to mental prayer, allow themselves to be lulled into nebulous reveries, to pity themselves, and fall asleep in the sweet warmth of vague pious emotions. They never succeed in focusing their minds on anything, because they are incapable of concentration. If they would only listen to and follow the curate's advice! But perhaps they would spurn it either out of pride or spiritual sloth, because they imagine that they are further advanced in the paths of mental prayer, or because they refuse to make the necessary effort.

I thought I could give no better answer to your recent letter, than to relate my conversation with the Trappist monk. You, too, want to learn how to pray. Why don't you listen to the Parisian curate's advice, and put it into practice?

A day will come when you will no longer need any words for your mental prayer. If I dare say so, you will have attained proficiency in the trade. Or more precisely, grace will have advanced its work in you. But don't try to rush forward. For the moment, "Speak to Him."

4. The advice of the old parish priest

I recently met a Savoyard peasant who, in addition to his regular work, has assumed heavy responsibilities in agricultural organizations. I had been told of the rather extraordinary influence he had on others as a Christian. We met and talked to each other about our respective activities. When I spoke to him about the *Cahiers sur l'oraison*, his interest visibly doubled. Sensing that his reaction intrigued me, he volunteered to satisfy my curiosity.

* * *

"When I was young, I often served the Mass of our old pastor. He was a strange man, rough, surly, silent; a man we feared a little, and loved, or rather revered, very much. We hesitated to turn to him about ordinary matters of daily life, but when we were in trouble we went at once to consult him at his rectory, which was more austere than a monk's cell.

"He spent hours on end in prayer at the church. One day, when I was about fourteen, I said to him, 'Father, I'd like to know how to pray, too.' My words must have had an extraordinary effect on him, because he smiled in a way that can't be put into words—and he was a man nobody had ever seen smiling.

"I have since speculated that he had been praying all his life that some day someone would ask him that question. He looked so happy, that I thought he was going to talk to me for a long time, right there in the sacristy filled with the vague scent of incense. Unfortunately, I can't find words to describe his clear-eyed look, his look of intense purity. But I can at least give you his answer verbatim. It was very short: 'When you go to God, lad, think very hard that he is there, and say to him, "Lord, I place myself at your service." ' And then, in his ordinary surly tone, he continued, 'Come now, hurry and put your cassock away.' I later came to understand that his abrupt manner was really a form of bashfulness.

"That day, I learned how to pray. And it will soon be forty years that I have practiced mental prayer by placing myself at God's service."

* * *

Come now, admit this story is worth a whole conference on mental prayer, and dispense me from writing you at greater length today. But try to understand what it means to be at God's service. It has far-reaching implications. We must first give up our right to dispose of ourselves. We must surrender totally to God, entrusting ourselves to his discretionary power—and that includes our body, our intellect, our heart, our will, our very life—so that he may dispose of us as he pleases.

But what's the use of trying to explain? Words are powerless to make one understand. Pray to the old pastor (who must not be surly any more, now that he has found the One whom he was seeking), that he may obtain for you the grace to be totally at God's service.

5. Being present to God

I share your impression that your spiritual life has now reached a plateau. After reflecting and praying, I came to the conclusion that that's the way things are going to be, as long as you do not make a larger place for prayer in your life. And by prayer, I mean essentially what is usually referred to as *mental prayer*. It used to be called "oraison," from the Latin *"oratio."*

For the Romans, *"orare"* meant addressing a prayer to the gods, pleading a cause, and, in a derived sense, making a discourse. Mental prayer is a conversation of the soul with God. That is the way spiritual men and women have always understood it. Clement of Alexandria wrote, "I dare say that mental prayer is a conversation with God." For St. Benedict, it is "attending to God." For St. Teresa of Avila, mental prayer is "a friendly exchange in which one converses in a tête-à-tête with this God by whom one knows he is loved." For Dom Marmion, it is "A talk between the child of God and his heavenly Father, under the guidance of the Holy Spirit."

These words "conversation" and "talk" involve the risk, however, of encouraging a certain ambiguity, because they give one to believe that mental prayer consists essentially in speaking inwardly to God. Now, mental prayer is a vital action that involves our whole being.

There is an expression which, if it is given its true depth of meaning, could translate quite well the interior action of the man or woman who is praying: being present to God. To help you grasp my thought, allow me to call to mind an event that must have remained very vivid in your memory.

I had come to pay you a visit. As you opened the door, you informed me that your daughter Monica probably had meningitis, and you led me to her room plunged in semi-darkness. Your wife was sitting next to the little bed, silent, intensely attentive to her child's poor emaciated face. At times, she would gently push a lock of hair from Monica's forehead. When the child opened her eyes, she responded by smiling—the kind of smile that words cannot describe.

Whatever the mother did, whether she was tidying things up in the room or taking a hasty meal in the neighboring room, she remained intensely present to her daughter. Every fiber of her being, every second of her life, was directed toward Monica.

That's the way it is, or at least should be, with mental prayer. It should be a profound attention of the soul, an exchange that goes beyond words which, without neglecting to speak, consists of something very different—an attention, a presence to God of one's whole being, body and soul, of all one's keenly alert faculties.

Do I need to take more time to plead the cause of mental prayer with you? I have every reason to think that the cause is already won, that you are not among the many Christians who refuse to admit the need for it. I shall not hide from you that I have a bad conscience when I need to multiply arguments in order to invite the sons of God to come close to their Father, to open their hearts to his revelations, to live in his close friendship, to express their love and gratitude to him.

How strange that there is a need to insist, so that beings endowed with understanding may strive to know the Something that is most interesting of all. So that beings created for love may come to love the Something that is most lovable. So that free beings may place themselves at the Lord's service, rather than at the service of his vassals. So that beings created for Happiness may not be content with small pleasures.

6. *"Speak, Lord, for your servant is listening"*
(1 S 3:9)

D o you remember what you were telling me one day about Philip? "He is a very obliging boy, always ready to do my errands. Sometimes he is so eager that he rushes off before even knowing what he is supposed to buy." As I was reading your last letter, I thought, "You are unmistakably his mother!"

When the time for your daily mental prayer arrives, you go about it without delay. Like Philip, you charge ahead. You think of God, you speak to God, and you try to make your love for him surge up, before you have even asked him what he is expecting, what he is hoping from you.

Now, I have no intention of addressing lofty thoughts on mental prayer to you. I want simply to give you some very modest advice, indeed advice as important as it is modest: never begin your mental prayer without first coming to a halt, taking a few moments to make silence within you, and asking what you should be doing during this quarter-hour of prayer.

I come back to your Philip. This obliging boy is also well-bred. I have noticed that when he is in the presence of what we call "grown-ups," he is silent. He lets them talk—even if he is itching to talk himself. Why, then, in the presence of the infinitely greater Being who is God, do you not do what you have taught your son to do? Why do you not give God the initiative in the conversation?

Please understand my advice. I am not suggesting that you ask yourself what you are going to say to God. On the contrary, you should ask him what he has to say to you, what answer he is expecting from you, and what attitude of soul on your part will be pleasing to him.

I know that you will retort, "Don't take me for some great mystic. I never hear God talk to me!" And for a good reason. In order to hear, one should perhaps begin by listening! "But there have been times when I didn't do all the talking, and even then I never perceived his voice." Is it so certain that you wanted to hear him, that you were listening with undivided attention?

Besides, I do not promise that God's voice will be perceptible to your senses, although that could happen. When St. Paul was fearful and depressed, and as though lost in the great cosmopolitan city of Corinth, he heard Christ's voice consoling him with great tenderness: *"Do not be afraid. Go on speaking and do not be silenced, for I am with you"* (Ac 18:9-10). But that is not the Lord's usual way of acting, even with St. Paul.

If you get into the habit of beginning your mental prayer with a moment of attentive, questioning silence, you will soon discover in what sense we can say that God speaks to us. Sometimes a thought will gently rise from this silence, a thought that has the savor of a prayer. Welcome it, and offer it a favorable climate in which to ripen. Call to mind the admirable verses of Paul Valéry, which we are not forbidden to apply to mental prayer:

* * *

Patience, patience,
Patience in the blue!
Every atom of silence
Is the chance for a ripe fruit!

* * *

At other times, thoughts will not appear as spontaneously. You will have to link your reflection to the silence, and search out what your mental prayer must be in order to answer the Lord's expectations.

For example, you will gaze in spirit at the perfections of this God in whose presence you are standing, and then maybe you will sense an imperious need to adore, to give thanks or to humble yourself.

Or else you will remember that the Spirit of Christ in the depths of your soul cries out, "Father! Father!", and your mental prayer will become a cleaving, in total faith, of your whole being to the love of the Son for his Father.

Or again, an event in the family or in the world will loom up to inspire your mental prayer, and you will intercede for those who need help, the way Abraham did by the oaks of Mamre, as he pleaded for the cities threatened with fire from the sky (cf. Gn 18:1 ff.).

It may seem to you that God did not really intervene in all of this, that you alone sought and chose the subject of your prayer. Truly, if you did not rush thoughtlessly into mental prayer, if you humbly asked the Lord to help you, it is permissible to think that he sustained your effort at reflection from within even if you were unaware of it, and brought you to an understanding of his thoughts and desires. When we communicate our thoughts and desires to another, aren't we talking to him?

In any event, always remain humble. Do not imitate those who naively imagine that every idea that comes to them indubitably is the thought of God himself.

From what I am writing you, remember above all that the first words of our prayer—whether we are beginners or are experienced in the life of mental prayer—must always be those of the young Samuel. *"Speak, Lord, for your servant is listening"* (1 S 3:9).

Father Bourgoing, who wrote back in the 17th century, dealt with the subject I have just been discussing with you. To support his thesis, he proposed an irresistible (!) argument: "If nature has given us two ears and only one tongue, it is to show that when we converse with men we must listen at least twice as much as we talk. How much more we should do this in our relations with God!"

7. An invention of love

"How is it that after fifteen years of regular mental prayer, I now find it so dull, so apparently ineffective, devoid of light and joy?"

To answer your question, I passed in review the explanations that spiritual writers have given for aridity in mental prayer. These include a life of faith that is insufficiently nourished by reading and meditation (especially the reading and meditation of the Word of God), and a tepid life of charity resulting from a failure to deliberately mortify one's inclinations, attachments, and passions. It can also be the result of a failure to discipline one's imagination and thinking.

But I am focusing more on another explanation. Without claiming, of course, that it is the correct one, I would like you to reflect on it at some length.

I wonder if you are not the victim of both routine and proficiency. When you decided to practice mental prayer, you were aware of your ignorance, and so you sought advice and read articles or books on the subject. I remember your eagerness to learn. As a result, each period of mental prayer was a victory over inexperience, apathy, and distractions. Or at least a courageous struggle.

Since then, you have acquired experience and proficiency. You know that it is very useful to prepare your mental prayer and to begin it well, and so you never fail to do these things. You struggle against distractions, but without tension, like an experienced man who knows that they are often permitted by God. You speak to the Lord, but you also know how to be silent, having discovered the price of silence in mental prayer. You are suffering because you no longer experience (as you once did) those sudden bursts of light and love, but you have learned that "aridity" has its place in every spiritual life that is advancing.

Have you not become a "professional" in mental prayer, who knows the rules of the art very well and applies them? We say of an artisan that he has a skillful hand. Speaking of a practitioner, a pianist, or a preacher, we say: he is a professional. That is certainly very important. But it is not enough, especially in man-to-man relations. I am thinking now of professors, writers, preachers, etc.

And it is certainly even less adequate in the relations between man and woman, within the home. I picture a young husband who has been taught that it is not good to improvise his evening conversations with his spouse. Armed with this advice, he comes home from the office and questions his wife on her day, her tasks, her encounters, and on the development of their newborn baby. For his part, he does not fail to tell her about the salient facts relating to his life at work. Then he suggests that they spend the evening reading together the book he has just bought. And yet, for all these sound ideas and praiseworthy efforts, the evening may turn out to be disappointing for them both, each one remaining solitary and bored, continuing his or her interior mono-logue, or perhaps escaping into some reverie.

The reason is that, in the domain of married life, it is not simply a matter of knowing the theory or of having acquired certain skills. Two living beings are never today what they were yesterday. They must set out each day toward their mutual encounter by unknown paths, and try to guess what is going on deep within the other's life. They must seek what can gain the other's attention, interest, and affection, and avoid for the moment whatever annoys or bores, while they search for the magnet that can establish communion between them. And then some-times the miracle happens! A genuine exchange in depth, in which two hearts and souls commune. Words are found that are wonderfully suited to enhance the exchange—unless silence achieves it better.

It is not enough to be well-versed in psychology, to know by heart the code of good relations between husband and wife. There is the need to invent every conversation, every evening together, so that it may be a real encounter. Now, it is hard and tiresome to invent. Or more precisely, it demands a young, vibrant love that is never resigned to mediocrity in conversations, but is impatient for closer communion, spurred by hope. It is love that elicits inventiveness, and reciprocal inventiveness enriches love.

What is true of married life is true also of mental prayer, because it, too, is a person-to-person encounter. Mental prayer deteriorates when savoir-faire takes the place of inventiveness. I wonder if this might not be the case with you. Indeed, it is very useful to know and to put into practice—as you are doing—the rules that men and women of prayer have taught us. But if the faculty of inventiveness does not come into play, then in spite of all this knowledge, mental prayer will remain polished, superficial, and artificial. It will not culminate in a communion of the soul with God.

You will tell me that a man who loves his wife can guess by signs imperceptible to anyone else—a certain smile, a gleam in her eye, a slight quiver of her face or hand—what brings joy to her heart.

But with God? Faith teaches us what pleases him. True, faith does not suffice to inform us as to what pleases him here and now, what he wants from this particular half hour of mental prayer. Is he expecting us to pause and reflect on a certain facet of his thought, or on one of his perfections? Does he want from us a particular attitude of soul, such as praise or repentance, adoration or filial trust? Does he want a change in an attitude which raises up a barrier between him and ourselves?

By what sign can we understand what God wants? It may be a quality of silence or peace, following anxiety (I am using the word in its etymological sense of absence of interior calm), or perhaps an impression of fulfillment. We sometimes have the feeling of having found a good attitude of soul. As I write this, a memory from my distant childhood comes to mind (forgive the laughable comparison): I see a billiard table, billiard balls on the table, and holes with numbers on them: 10, 100, 500, 1,000. The trick was to place the balls in the holes with the largest numbers. The balls rolled and gained momentum. One ball would approach a hole and then move away from it, and finally fall into another, quivering for a few instants and finally settling down, its calm restored.

So when we have trouble getting our mental prayer started, it is a good idea to "try" successively some thoughts or attitudes of soul that have helped us to pray during an earlier period of mental prayer. If none of these awakens a response or a feeling of peace in us, we will remain unstable, as it were, more or less anxious. We have to keep searching, knowing that our very effort is already pleasing to God.

On the other hand, if peace settles in our soul, if we have the impression of being in the truth, then we can stop searching. We have found what God wanted of us. There is the need only to gently penetrate deeper into the thought, or to strengthen our attitude. Thanks to the gifts of the Holy Spirit, little by little we shall become better able to discern what pleases God.

Even if we remain in uncertainty, we are on the right path, provided our mental prayer is governed by the will to respond to God's expectations. Let us search gropingly, but always peacefully, conversing with God as a son talks with his Father.

The thing to remember out of this long letter is that each of your times of mental prayer must be an invention of love—I mean an invention in the sense of discovery—a discovery of what is pleasing to God. The memory of what yesterday's mental prayer was like, or the mere knowledge of an art of praying, will not teach you what today's mental prayer must be. You have to search with the flexibility of a fully awakened, industrious, hopeful soul.

8. The essential

Y ou write: "I have been faithful to daily mental prayer for more than six months, but I am not sure of having had more than four or five good sessions of mental prayer." What do you mean? That all of your mental prayer, outside those four or five sessions, failed to please the Lord? You don't know. That they did not give you personal satisfaction? I am willing to believe that. But does it follow that they were not good? I beg of you, don't fall into this trap that awaits all beginners, of judging your mental prayer according to fervor, recollection, beautiful ideas, or tangible results. The same is true of mental prayer as of the sacraments: its value and efficacy are of the supernatural order, and hence escape our human measurements.

If you had really grasped the essential element of mental prayer, you would not have become discouraged by what you call "the assault of distractions."

Mental prayer is a complex action. The whole of a man enters into it: body, soul, intellect, heart, and freedom. But it is important to clearly discern the essential, for when this is lacking, mental prayer loses all value.

Could it be the part played by the body? Obviously not. Otherwise, we would have to say that a paralytic cannot pray, because he cannot adopt proper physical attitudes for prayer. That would be absurd.

Does the essential consist in words? It is all too evident that words, in prayer as well as in human relations, can never be the essential.

Is the essential, sensitivity or fervor? That's very deceiving, for it takes such a trifle to perturb sensitivity: a worry, a sorrow, a joy, a passion, a toothache. Really, the value of our mental prayer cannot possibly be at the mercy of the slightest event, whether interior or exterior.

Or does it lie in reflections? Certainly meditation is important: knowledge of God elicits love for God. But if this were the essential of mental prayer, the person not well-endowed intellectually would be condemned to mediocre mental prayer, since perfection would be reserved to highly intelligent persons.

Or is attention to God essential? If it is, then you will sink into despair, since you are under the assault of "distractions." For it is very often beyond our power to eliminate them. Our attention, like our sensitivity, is especially unstable. It is just as hard to keep our attention turned toward God, as it is to keep the needle of a compass fixed toward the north while we are walking.

Well then, what is left? The emotions—an ardent love, a lively trust, a deeply-felt gratitude? Now, it is true that our emotions, by comparison with our sensitivity and imagination, give evidence of a certain stability. Even so, we must admit that they are in part beyond our control. We cannot command them. The heart's fervor does not depend on our decision.

What, then, is the essential of prayer? It lies in the will. But don't think of the will as the psychological mechanism through which we make decisions, or as that which constrains us to perform acts that displease us. In sound philosophical parlance, the will is the aptitude of our innermost being to freely turn toward a good, toward a person, or an ideal. Let us call it the aptitude to "commit ourselves," to use a word dear to our generation. It is when our innermost being turns toward God, and surrenders itself to him freely and deliberately, that there is true prayer. This is so even if our sensitivity is dormant, our reflections meager, and our attention distracted. Our prayer is worth as much as this fundamental orientation and self-giving.

Whereas our sensitivity, our attention, and even our emotions are fleeting and changing, our will is infinitely more stable and permanent. The agitations of sensitivity do not involve our will. The distractions of our imagination are not necessarily distractions of the will. I appeal to your own experience. During mental prayer, has it never happened that, suddenly aware of being carried away by distractions, you turned inward and recovered your calm and tenacious will orientated toward God, and eager to please him? In your will, nothing had changed.

To want to pray is to pray. I am well aware that this formula has the gift of irritating those of our contemporaries who nurture the superstition of spontaneity. In their eyes, everything that we demand of ourselves is artificial, conventional, and false. But I know you well enough to realize that you are not inclined to such infantilism.

Ideally, of course, prayer that wells up from our innermost will should galvanize our whole being. In fact, nothing about us should remain a stranger to our prayer—any more than to our love. God wants all of us: *"You shall love the Lord your God with all your heart, with all your soul, with all your mind, and with all your strength"* (Mk 12:30). That is why we must strive to banish parasitical noises and activities, collect ourselves, and gather ourselves up totally, so as to offer ourselves totally. But, I repeat, it is fortunately not necessary that we succeed in doing this, for our mental prayer to be of good quality.

Anyone who wants to overcome distractions and agitation, must depend more on divine grace than on his own efforts. It is nonetheless true that it is good to know and to practice a few classical rules:

- An old-time writer (somewhat of a misogynist) taught: "Distractions in mental prayer are like women. Pay no attention to them and they will soon leave you alone!!"

- To be grieved for having been distracted is another way of being distracted.
- To include the thought that comes to mind in one's agenda sometimes suffices to be rid of it: the telephone call that one must not fail to make during the day, etc.
- To choose the hour least favorable to distractions; for many this is the first hour of the day.
- To write out one's prayer, to help the mind fix its attention when it is too agitated.
- To make of one's distractions subjects of mental prayer: one's grown son whose faith is wavering, etc.

9. The practice of mental prayer

I am not going to talk to you about methods of mental prayer, as you have asked me to do. You will easily find them in any treatise on prayer. I want only to give you a little advice on your practice of mental prayer.

Don't look for anything original in this letter. I shall be content to present to you the classical advice that the spiritual writers give to those who have decided to practice mental prayer. But be sure not to see their counsels as recipes guaranteed to "work." Seek rather to grasp the spirit of what they are saying.

An image comes to mind that brings back memories long gone, of the time when I was young. We were runners, toeing the line, straining forward, all our muscles taut and ready to be released. The same holds true for mental prayer as for racing: it is important to get off to a good start. If we fail to do this, after five minutes we are quite surprised to find ourselves on a prie-dieu. While our body came to prayer, our thoughts have remained absorbed with secular concerns.

I strongly urge you, therefore, to take special care about your gestures and attitude when you begin your mental prayer. These include a well-made genuflection, which is an act of the soul as well as of the body; the alert and vigorous attitude of a wide-awake man present to himself and to God; a sign of the cross, made slowly and filled with meaning. A certain deliberateness and calm are very important in breaking the tense and rapid rhythms of a busy and hurried life like yours. So are a few moments of silence. Like a foot on the brake, they will help to introduce you into the rhythms of mental prayer and effect the necessary rupture with your preceding activities. It may also be a good idea to recite a vocal prayer very slowly in a low voice.

Then become aware, not of the presence of God, so much as of God present. A living being, the Great Living Being, is there waiting for you. He sees you and loves you. He has his ideas about this prayer that is beginning, and he asks you to agree blindly with what he expects of it.

Watch over your interior attitudes even more than over your bodily attitudes. The fundamental attitudes of man vis-a-vis God are dependence and repentance.

Dependence: Not the vague submission of someone who must sometimes renounce one of his plans in order to do God's will, but a far more radical dependence—the dependence of the torrent (that annihilates itself if it cuts itself off from the wellspring), of the vine-shoot (that dries up and rots when it is separated from the vine stock), and of the human body (that is no longer a body but a corpse, when the bond that joined it to the soul is broken).

Repentance: The acute sign of our basic unworthiness in the presence of the Holiness of God. Like St. Peter, who suddenly prostrates himself before Christ: *"Leave me, Lord. I am a sinful man"* (Lk 5:8).

These two attitudes are important to smooth the paths of the Lord within you.

When your soul is thus disposed, ask for the grace of mental prayer. For, as I have already told you, mental prayer is a gift from God before it is an activity of man. Humbly call upon the Holy Spirit, for it is he who teaches us to pray.

You can then adopt the bodily posture you find most favorable for freedom of soul. When the body threatens to drag the soul down into its laxness or torpor, stay awake and alert. At other times, lest your body, in its fatigue or tenseness, demand attention the whole time, grant it a posture of rest and relaxation.

Once prepared in this way, mental prayer in the strict sense can begin. You should expect nothing less, than that God will take possession of you. The only means to this end is to galvanize the three great supernatural faculties of faith, hope and charity. These are called *theological* virtues, because the Lord gave them to us that we may come in contact, in communion, with him. They are supernatural dynamisms within us, ready to go into action the instant we come to God.

Exercise your faith. I do not ask you to speculate about God. Meditate on what he tells you about himself through Creation (in which everything speaks of his perfections), through the Bible, and above all through his Son, who became man for the sake of revealing to us the infinite love of the Father. It is the great merit of St. Bernard, of the Franciscans of the 13th and 14th centuries, and of St. Ignatius of Loyola, to have reminded prayerful souls that Jesus Christ is, if we dare say so, *the* great subject of meditation.

The important thing is not to think a great deal, but to love much. Since faith has set charity in motion, exercise charity. Once again, I have used the term "exercise." Make no mistake about it. I am not extolling an unbridled voluntarism. The exercise of faith and charity should be as natural and relaxed as breathing. The exercise of charity consists, not so much in calling forth emotions, fervors, and sentiments, as in cleaving with all your will to God himself, espousing his desires and his interests.

It is also the hallmark of love to aspire to union with the beloved—and to the happiness this union promises. Where God is concerned, this aspiration is called "hope." I therefore urge you to exercise hope.

What I have just described is called "theological mental prayer." It is sometimes slandered as if it were a rich man's pastime. If we were to believe its detractors, it is suitable for monks, but not for those embroiled in the harsh combats of action. But take note! We must also be concerned with efficacy, they say. We could respond that praise and adoration take precedence over action. Even on the level of efficacy, where they take their stand, mental prayer is easily defended. The Scholastics of an earlier age used to say, "One acts according to one's being." Since theological prayer is a prodigious renewal of our being, placing it once again in contact with its Creator, it multiplies our efficiency. We need only read the lives of the saints, such as St. Teresa of Avila's, for example, to be convinced that this is so.

To extol theological mental prayer is not, however, to condemn what is known as "practical mental prayer." Indeed, there is every reason to harmonize and combine them.

It is crystal clear that we need to reform our lives, and reflect on our affections, thoughts, and behavior, in order to correct them. That is precisely the purpose of "practical mental prayer." Why should this not be the ordinary conclusion of a theological mental prayer? After contemplating God with the eyes of faith, we would turn our gaze on our own life. Charity, after renewing our intimacy with God, would impel us to serve him in our daily tasks. One of my friends never ends his mental prayer without what he calls "meditation on the agenda." He thinks about his coming day, and presents it to the Lord. He enumerates the persons he is to meet, and his enumeration becomes an intercession.

When you have finished reading this letter, are you going to think that mental prayer is an exercise that is not simple at all, that is discouraging for those whose lives are already so complicated? Do not linger over this impression. The most vital acts appear complicated when we analyze them—going down a flight of stairs, breathing, loving. But for those who are adept at them, they are very simple indeed.

It is precisely the word "simplicity" that designates a form of mental prayer to which those who persevere attain: "the prayer of simplicity." Father Grou describes it in this way:

* * *

"Instead of the complicated and fatiguing exercise of the memory, the understanding, and the will, which are at work in meditation, first on one subject and then on another, God often introduces the soul to a simple prayer in which the mind has no other object than a general vision of God; the heart, no other sentiment than a sweet and peaceful taste for God that nourishes the soul without effort, the way milk nourishes children. The soul is then so little aware of its operations, so subtle and delicate are they, that it has the sense of being idle, and plunged in a kind of sleep."

* * *

I shall add a final comment before taking leave of you. Just as one cannot become a cabinetmaker, a musician, or a writer overnight, so, too, one does not become a man of prayer without a laborious apprenticeship. To be surprised at this, one must have a very poor idea of what prayer is. He must never have entered the confines of a monastery, and seen young men who did not hesitate to leave everything in order to be initiated into prayer. He must have never encountered old monks, whose gentle, limpid gaze discloses much about the secrets of their life of prayer.

10. Mental prayer, a gift from God

G od asks me to believe, and I try to; to love my neighbor, and I strive to; to be pure, and I struggle to succeed in it. This is the spontaneous reaction of many Christians. It is touching, and is a proof of good will and generosity. And yet, it is very simplistic, the sign of a faith that is still puerile. It is ignorant of the truth, present in all of Scripture, that without God's help, man is powerless to please him or come up to his expectations.

Belief in Christ is impossible, if God does not intervene. *"No one can come to me unless the Father who sent me draws him"* (Jn 6:44). Love is impossible for us, unaided. St. Paul tells us that it is the Holy Spirit who pours charity into our hearts. Purity, too, must be received from the Lord. *"A clean heart create for me, O God"* (Ps 51:12). The same is true for prayer. Do you think about that?

You understood that you had to make a place for mental prayer in your life. You are practicing it, but you are not succeeding very well. And so, you blame yourself for lacking in skill, in will, and in perseverance. Should you not rather blame yourself for lacking an adult faith? Don't you depend entirely too much on yourself alone? You want to engage in mental prayer? Then ask God for the grace of mental prayer. Yes, indeed! Let your prayer consist in asking for prayer. Prayer, the flame that rises up within us toward God, is something we must ask for, just as Elijah called down fire from heaven on the wood he had just stacked up. Ask with perseverance and humility. Ask impatiently and importunely. Do not forget that Christ praised the importunate friend, the man who does not give up until he has won his case.

"My Father is at work until now, and I am at work as well" (Jn 5:17)

In the encounter of love that is mental prayer, God is the principal actor. That is why we must begin by believing that his love is eager to respond to our expectations, and why we must offer ourselves to its action.

Why thrash about so much, as if the value of our prayer were measured entirely by our efforts? God's love encompasses us, and presses upon us from all sides. We need only open all the doors and windows of our being.

11 *Believing in the Sun*—Mental prayer is the work of God with the cooperation of man, and not the reverse. What we must do, is surrender the depths of our being to God's action.

12 *The fable of the violin and the violinist*—Mark the Evangelist says of Jesus, facing the rich young man: "Jesus looked at him with love" (Mk 10:21). That is true for each one of us. To pray is to become aware of this look of love, and to offer ourselves to its purifying and regenerative power.

13 *"He looked at him with love"* (Mk 10:21)—God looks at us, because he is thinking about us. He looks at us with love, because he thinks of us with love. He has been doing this from all eternity. This thought of God is what brought us into being and maintains us. It is this thought, too, that will call into being the unique saint that each of us is called to become, if we do not resist him.

14 *If God stopped thinking about me*—Could our sinfulness make the Lord turn his eyes away from us? Certainly not, since it is not our holiness that attracts his love. Indeed, it is his love that makes pure,

alive, and holy the one who believes in him with unshakable faith.

15 *"I will become a torrent"*—This love from which no being is excluded is not, however, an impersonal love poured out indiscriminately on all humans. God loves each of his children with a unique love.

16 *Because I'm Agnes*—That is why he wants to be actively responsible for us.

17 *I take you in my care*—Through our prayers of petition, we go out to meet his love, impatient to work for our happiness and our holiness.

18 *You are asking me too timidly*—We must reject all timidity, and approach him with the boldness of a child who knows that he is loved, infinitely loved, and dares believe everything and hope for everything.

19 *Filial assurance*—What makes our prayer all-powerful with God Almighty, is that it is the work of the Holy Spirit himself acting within us.

20 *"Abba, Father!"*

11. Believing in the Sun

You are running up against the classical obstacle: the feeling of getting nowhere, of wasting time at mental prayer. Perhaps—who knows?—you feel the secret humiliation of offering God only a formless, desperately empty prayer. And you are already discouraged. Are you forgetting that you are not alone in your mental prayer, that God is there with you? You must not judge the value of this time of prayer solely from the point of view of your own activity. God acts too, and acts first. His action may well be more important than yours!

When you are sunbathing, you do not need to scurry about to get the sun to warm and penetrate you. You need only to be there, offered to the sun's rays. The same is true of prayer: we need only to expose ourselves to the Sun.

But we must believe in the Sun and in its action. It is our faith that matters. It alone perceives the sanctifying action of God, and opens us up and surrenders us to this action.

So never begin your mental prayer without taking cognizance of God present to you, and offer yourself to his active and efficacious love.

And persevere: it is because of your perseverance that God will transform you and divinize you, little by little.

If you are tempted to lose heart, look at the end point to which fidelity to mental prayer has brought the saints. The powerful desire that impelled you to walk toward God, the desire for a very intimate union with him, will reawaken. Look! Here's a passage from St. John of the Cross. It can restore your courage:

> "In thus allowing God to work in it, the soul . . . is at once illumined and transformed in God, and God communicates to it His supernatural Being, in such wise that it appears to be God Himself, and has all that God Himself has.
> . . . all the things of God and the soul are one in participant transformation; and the soul seems to be God rather than a soul, and is indeed God by participation; although it is true that its natural being, though thus transformed, is as distinct from the Being of God as it was before, even as the window has likewise a nature distinct from that of the ray, though the ray gives it brightness."*

12. The fable of the violin and the violinist

The audition is over. There is loud applause as the curtain falls. It redoubles in enthusiasm. The violin comes to the front of the stage, bows, and pointing to the timid violinist standing in the wings, addresses the public: "I hope that your applause is for the gentleman as much as for me. I owe it to the truth to acknowledge that, without his collaboration, I would not have done so well."

There are many Christians who make me think of this violin! Are you perhaps one of them? For them, holiness—toward which they are striving with great good will—is the work of man with God's collaboration. Their ways of acting are revealing on this point. For instance, their prayer consists in asking God for his help, and pleading their cause with him by means of all the good arguments they can muster, so as to make him decide to intervene in their favor. Such a frame of mind is no doubt touching, but it rests on an infantile conception of the relationship between God and man. It distorts Christian life, and impedes the soul's journey toward perfection. As a matter of fact, sanctification is not

* *Ascent of Mount Carmel,* Book 2, Chapter 5, Paragraph 7, in volume one of *The Complete Works of St. John of the Cross,* translated and edited by E. Allison Peers, Newman Press, 1935, 1964.

man's work with the help of God, but God's work with the help of man. And that is something very different.

When we understand this, everything is transformed, and our mental prayer first of all. Our prayer no longer focuses on getting God to decide to act, or getting him to take an interest in his child. We have finally grasped that God is always acting, as our Lord has said: *"My Father and I are always at work"* (cf. Jn 5:17). Mental prayer consists essentially in surrendering ourselves to this divine action.

Of course, it is possible to find a way of remaining in a state of surrender from morning until night, but often our activities loosen the bonds that join us to God. They thus tend to pull us out of the range of his action. It is through mental prayer that we come back to it, and surrender our whole being, with all of its faculties, to his control. And once back to our tasks, we remain within the orbit of God's action. Led by the Spirit of God, we then act as sons of God. In the words of St. Paul, *"All who are led by the Spirit of God are sons of God"* (Rm 8:14).

In this perspective, your prayers will not be the petitions of a child trying to force the Lord's hand, teasing to make him change his mind. Rather, they will be a conversion (the word comes from the Latin *convertere*: to turn towards), a turning around of your being to become humble, receptive, and pervious to the Lord's sanctifying action. It is not a question of getting God to be converted to us, but indeed of our being converted to him.

13. *"He looked at him with love"* (cf. Mk 10:21)

The Gospels make mention several times of Christ's looking at certain persons. Andrew presented his brother Simon to Jesus, and Jesus *"looked at him"* (Jn 1:42). Peter had just denied his Master. *"The Lord turned around and looked at Peter"* (Lk 22:61). Peter went out and wept bitterly. A virtuous man asked Christ the way to eternal life. Mark tells us, with his gift for brief and evocative formulas, *"Jesus looked at him with love"* (Mk 10:21).

Love and looking go hand in hand. One must look in order to love, but one must also love in order to really look. "We see clearly only with the heart."

Nothing reveals love better than the look in our eyes. The person who is the object of such a look makes no mistake about it. His or her whole being—I am speaking of the inner being, the secret self—is awakened, quivers, is filled with wonder, and goes forth and lives under the shock of this look of love. A new, unknown, ardent, intense life rises up within him or her. The look of love inspires love.

The most wonderful thing about another's looking at us with love, is not only what we discover in this look about the soul and the love of this other person, but what we learn about ourselves. This look of love is actually a "mirror in which one sees oneself being seen," to use the apt formula of Lanza del Vasto.

There are looks in which we see ourselves as contemptible, as some trifling quantity. When we are looked at with love, we discover that we are lovable in the strongest sense of the word, capable of arousing love in the heart of another. A mirror such as this tells us about ourselves, but not the way an inanimate and impassible mirror does. It speaks to us through the joy, astonishment, love, and élan awakened in this other being at the sight of our inner self, and which the look of the other reveals to us.

It is a deeply moving experience to discover that we are worthy of being loved, capable of making love well up in another's heart like a spring from a rock. How can we help being reconciled with ourselves? Love, esteem, self-respect—sentiments either unknown or at least scarcely burgeoning until then (and very often warped, at that), now spring up within us, and make us suddenly aware of our dignity. From that moment, we know that we have a reason for being, since we *exist for* someone else.

But there is something even more wonderful. This is the look of a Christian who discerns, in the light of Christ, that our innermost self is the soul of a child of God. He learns our eternal name spoken by God from all eternity—the name that brought us into being in the divine Mind before we were called into existence. This look has the very poignant quality of being completely transparent to God's own gaze at us, so that we discover in it the measure of God's love for us.

I am certain that God would want every man and woman to encounter such a look at least once in his or her life.

But even those who love us most cannot always be actively loving. Their looks of love—and I am speaking, above all, of the soul's gaze— are privileged and intermittent moments. Where God is concerned, we can be sure that he is always in the act of loving. This act, this fervent attention, is his presence of love to our soul.

Wonderment, too. Yes, God finds delight in the soul of his child, amazing as it may seem, because in this soul his gaze sees what is more real than its own being. He sees the soul's eternal divine name.

God's look of love is more efficacious than any human look. This divine gaze creates holiness, and is a communication of divine life.

If God's look of love is to produce its effects, the soul must be receptive, opening up its depths to it by an act of faith. This must be the faith of the man who acknowledges the love of his God for him—an active love, love in act. If this faith were fervent and not intermittent, God's look of love would never cease making the soul grow in holiness, just as the sun makes the crops ripen.

To pray is to become aware that God is looking at us with love. It is to open ourselves through faith to his creative, regenerative, divinizing and beatifying action. Then love for God, *charity*, wells up in the soul.

To pray well, we must believe that God looks with love at each and every one of us.

"He looked at him with love" (Mk 10:21).

14. If God stopped thinking about me

You ask: "Am I right to believe that if God stopped thinking about me for a single instant, I would cease to exist? Is that an error? I would be very sad if it were, because since this idea came to me one day during mental prayer, I have felt so much closer to the Lord. More precisely, I have sensed him so much closer to me."

Have no fear at all. What you have understood is perfectly orthodox.

Everything that exists has been created by God, and is preserved in existence by him. Hence, nothing exists that is not *willed* by him—willed not once and for all, but at every instant. So, there is nothing that has not been *thought* by him, since nothing can be willed unless it has first been thought. If God ceased to preserve a being in existence, this being would immediately fall back into non-existence. The same would happen if he stopped willing it or thinking of it.

Now I hope that you are completely reassured. You should note, however, that while it is not an error to distinguish between thought, will, and act in God, we must understand that this is a human way of speaking. God thinks, wills, and acts in one selfsame action.

I can clearly grasp this sentiment of God's proximity that your "idea" awakened in you. When someone thinks about us, he or she becomes more present to us than through physical proximity. The latter can only be corporeal. I am reminded of a wife living with a husband who is no more present to her, than if he were living at the antipodes. Presence and absence are first of all of the spiritual order.

But follow the truth you have glimpsed, to its ultimate conclusion. Understand that God has been thinking about you *for all eternity*. Your coming into existence was simply the realization in time of this eternal thought which is a thought of love. God had forever cherished this thought when he created you.

You incarnate God's thought. You are his thought, but in the embryonic state. Life is given to you—and grace is operating in you—so that it may attain its plenitude.

Indeed, God can think and will only a perfect being, one that has attained plenitude. The divine thought that you are, is therefore the thought of a saint, like no other saint, for two identical thoughts never spring up in God.

By cooperating with God's work within you, you will become the saint that God delighted in inventing from all eternity.

15. "I will become a torrent"

Your letter touched me deeply, especially this part: "Why don't you ever write for poor miserable sinners? Please have a little pity on those who cannot pray to God with the prayer of the just, and tell them if it is true that they are not excluded from the kingdom of prayer." I must have expressed myself very badly in my earlier letters, if I gave you to believe that they were the letters of a just man addressing other just men!

To begin with, I find it very difficult to accept your distinctions. Can anyone claim to be just? Is there anyone who is not a sinner? Who can attempt to pray without first confessing his sin, and avowing his repentance? And what wretchedness can discourage God?

I am reminded of a certain young woman who was extraordinarily beautiful and passionately loved. She was dismayed beyond words, when her surgeon gave her a most disturbing diagnosis of a tiny, harmless-looking pimple at the corner of her lip. If her beauty were impaired, would she still be loved?

The same sort of anxiety sometimes occurs in individuals aware of their moral ugliness. They can stop worrying. Even though it takes beauty or goodness to awaken love in a human heart, the same does not hold true for God. God's love is of an entirely different nature. St. Paul was well aware of this, and designated it by a word not currently used before him: *agape*, which has been translated by the word "charity."

It is not the sight of a creature's lovableness that arouses God's love. It is his own love that creates the lovableness, the beauty, and the goodness of the being he loves. Because we are sinners, we are distraught at having lost the moral beauty that earned for us the esteem of others (and above all, our own self-esteem), and we imagine that God also turns away from us. As if our virtue had won us his love up to now! As if man could capture God's esteem, or awaken his love!

God's love for us does not have its origin in us. Neither our virtues nor our wretchedness can influence God's love. His love is not motivated from outside himself. It is a spontaneous welling up, an overflowing of riches, a creative dynamism. God is not searching for human values to love. He is seeking out the poor man (in the Biblical sense of the term—the sinner, the fool, the weakling, the one in whom he finds a void to fill).

But the sinner is unaware of this quality of God's love, and thinks that God has made a mistake. Like St. Peter, he protests, *"Leave me, Lord. I am a sinful man"* (Lk 5:8). Well, God will not go away, and the sinner's wretchedness will become the monstrance of his Love.

This is why the sinner's prayer consists, above all, in an unshakable belief in this absolute gratuitousness of God's love, and in consenting to it without pusillanimity. It seems wonderfully simple, but often turns out to be very difficult. Our need to be loved by God for our own excellence is very deep-seated and tenacious. It is often unavowed, and unknown to ourselves. The proof of this is the bitter vexation that perturbs our interior life when we have succumbed to temptation.

In our relations with God, we must radically fight this tendency to see his love as the recognition of our own value. The reason God does not protect us from every failure is, no doubt, that he wants to oblige us to discover that his love for us is not based on our virtue, but springs spontaneously from his heart. He wants to make us realize that there is no danger that his love will undergo change, inasmuch as it does not depend on what he finds in us.

Our Lord used to say to St. Catherine of Siena, "Become a capacity to receive, and I will become a torrent." That's the prayer of the beggar, of the sinner. He must become a capacity to receive.

16. Because I'm Agnes

O nly those who know God pray well. If we want to pray more effectively, we must seek to know God better. He has taken care to direct our search, by revealing to us that he is Love. But what is this Love? Its reflection, in those who love us, enables us to glimpse it. By contrast, its caricature, in those who love us badly, also helps us to understand it better. Such has been the experience of a woman, abandoned by her husband, who has recently written to me. I am copying her letter for you. The possessive love of this husband for his wife, strangely enough, brings out the personal character and generosity of God's love.

H.C.

* * *

". . . He did not love me. He loved the woman in me, or more precisely, my femaleness. I was a specimen of femininity that was congenial to him. But when he discovered that I was 'somebody,' when he encountered my 'me,' he was annoyed, not knowing what to do with a 'me,' with a living person. From that moment, there was something in his life that was superfluous, cumbersome. Something, or rather somebody, who denied him the right to be alone, alone with a thing of his very own; somebody who affirmed rights, and first of all the right to be recognized as a unique, one-of-a-kind person. That was just too much. He backed away. It was as if he felt threatened in his own territory. He came to think of me as an intruder. I had taken the liberty to be a person, when he was asking me to be an inanimate object, a pleasant, comfortable specimen of femininity. He strayed. He looked elsewhere. And one day he found another woman who, at least so he thinks, is willing to be his 'thing.'

"After cruelly dark months, during which I alternated between rage and depression, when every possible temptation assailed me, I can no longer blame him. Today I am at peace, or rather I am possessed by peace.

"And I owe it all to him. Through my suffering as a badly loved wife, I was led to discover God's love for me. Now I know that God, for his part, does not love me as a little specimen of humanity because he loves 'humanity,' but because I'm Agnes. God is not like the sun, which gives forth its heat indiscriminately and impassibly to all creatures. God gives me his love, he gives me himself, *because I'm me*. God is not like a certain social worker who loves the poor, but never takes the time to look at each one of them in the eye, or to know the name of each person she is helping. What would be the use of it? What she loves is 'the poor.' God is not like that at all. He loves me, Agnes, and he loves me because I'm Agnes. He knows me by my eternal name. He calls me by my name. He is impatient for my answer. He is not jealous of my autonomy or of my personhood. They are dear to him. Of what value would my response be without them? For God, I am not a 'thing' which he preempts to be used, but a freedom that surrenders itself, and for which he has infinite respect.

"Thanks to God's love, I am reconciled with myself and with others. God has released the wellsprings of tenderness within my heart. Now at last I am living. And the hour of prayer is also the hour of most intense living for me. . . ."

17. I take you in my care

Y ou are quite right to be indignant at a certain way of speaking about God, which attributes to him purely human thoughts, sentiments, and modes of behavior. It is a serious error. It profanes the divine mystery, and in the last analysis lays the foundation for atheism. There are many believers all around us who surrender to it. It is nothing new. Voltaire was already denouncing it in a famous saying I cite to you from memory: "God made man in his own image, and man certainly returned the compliment."

On the other hand, you are wrong to relegate God to the mists of the unknowable. As if we had to be resigned to know nothing about him!

It is true that our *"God is hidden"* (Is 45:15). It is true that he is altogether different from us. He himself has declared it through the prophet Hosea: *"I am God and not man"* (Ho 11:9).

God is not in the image of man. Let us stoutly maintain it. But man is in the image of God. And that's why the qualities of man, especially his qualities of heart, give us an insight into the perfections of God's love for us.

The Bible vigorously and continuously affirms the transcendence of the Most High. It denies that the human intellect has the power to know the Creator the way one knows a creature. However, it does not hesitate to speak to us of God, by first speaking to us about creatures.

The Bible invites us to find in God the affection of a father *"who raises an infant to his cheeks"* (Ho 11:4); the tenderness of a mother: *"Can a mother forget her infant, be without tenderness for the child of her womb? Even should she forget, I will never forget you"* (Is 49:15); and the faithfulness of a husband: *"The Lord calls you back, like a wife . . . married in youth and then cast off, says your God. For a brief moment I abandoned you, . . . but with enduring love I take pity on you"* (Is 54:6-8).

It is a deeply religious attitude to discern, in God, the wellspring of the most delicate sentiments, the tenderest and most vehement feelings of the human heart.

In the last few days, I thought of you as I read a passage of Anouilh, which I am copying for you. In it, you will see the reaction of a husband in the presence of his young wife, who has fallen asleep from sheer exhaustion.

* * *

"It sufficed for you to stop talking, to let your head slip onto my shoulder, and it was all over. . . . The others continued to laugh and talk around me, but I had just bid them farewell. Young Jason was dead. I was your father and mother; I was the one who held the head of the sleeping Medea resting on him. What was your little woman's brain dreaming about, while I was thus taking you in my care? I carried you to our bed. . . . I just looked at you as you slept. The night was calm, we had long since outstripped your father's pursuers. My armed companions kept watch around us, and yet I did not dare close my eyes. I defended you, Medea— indeed against nothing at all—that whole night."

* * *

Try to understand—and this will be a wonderful consolation for you—that your God is no less "human" in your regard, when you happen to fall asleep during mental prayer in the evening at the end of a hard day's work. I know that you will not interpret this text as an invitation to laxity, but as a call to trust in the One who loves you more tenderly than a man cherishes his beloved, and who takes care of you with infinite solicitude.

18. You are asking me too timidly

Praise, adoration, abandonment to divine love—you tell me—are the great wellsprings of your mental prayer. I am delighted to know this. But don't neglect the prayer of petition, as if it were inferior, or a developmental stage that you have already passed. We must never abandon a single one of the so-called ends of prayer: adoration, thanksgiving, repentance, and petition. They make up the fabric of the Church's liturgy. They must likewise constitute the fabric of your private mental prayer.

I have often noticed that prayer of petition is a sure criterion by which to judge the authenticity of a spirituality. False mystics scorn it, true mystics delight in it. A saint is always a beggar, not necessarily at the door of men's houses, but at God's door. He takes pleasure in expecting his daily bread from the Lord. Above all, he begs from him the spiritual riches which he craves even more: an increase in the theological virtues, the knowledge and love of the Cross, humility, compunction, and the gifts of the Holy Spirit.

Besides, the truly spiritual person remembers the Master's saying that inspires us to this prayer of petition: *"There is more happiness in giving than receiving"* (Ac 20:35). He discovers in these words a secret of Christ's heart, and even more, a strict command and a confidential disclosure. It is this joy of giving that he wants to provide to his God, by becoming a petitioner before him.

Examine your own heart as a father. Does it not witness to the same thing?

I discovered an echo of this need to give and this joy in giving, in a letter of St. Thomas More to his daughter Margaret. In reading it, we clearly see that holiness does not eliminate paternal sentiments. Rather, it refines and deepens them so that they become, as it were, a mirror that reflects the sentiments of God. When you read this text, in which this admirable father expresses his need to give and his joy in giving, understand that in God your Father these feelings are far more vehement:

* * *

"You are too bashful and timid in your request for money, from a father who wants to give it and when you have greeted me with a letter such that I would not only repay each line of it with a gold Philippeus (as Alexander did with Choerilos), but, if my means were as great as my desire, I would reward each syllable with two ounces of gold. As it is, I send only what you have asked, but would have added more, except that as I am eager to give, so I like to be asked and coaxed by my daughter, especially by you, whom virtue and learning have made so dear to my heart. So the sooner you spend this money well, as you always do, and the sooner you ask for more, the more will you be sure of pleasing your father. Farewell, my dearest daughter."*

19. Filial Assurance

W hy have I treated you like a man of the Old Testament? Because you seem to be unaware of a virtue that is the hallmark of every true disciple of Christ, in his relations with God: filial assurance.

Devout Jews did not dare approach their God and speak to him freely. They adored him, but at a distance, as it were. They thought that they would be risking death if they heard Yahweh speak, and above all if they saw him. They addressed him as a dreaded and revered Master: *"O Lord, may your ear be attentive to my prayer and that of all willing servants who revere your name!"* (Ne 1:11).

Only the high priest had the right to pronounce the sacred tetragram, the four consonants of the divine Name. That was the utmost familiarity permitted. When those who stood around the high priest heard it, they prostrated themselves to the ground. The others said, "Praised be forever the Name of his glorious Reign." No one

---

* *St. Thomas More: Selected Letters*, edited by Elizabeth Frances Rogers, Yale University Press, 1961, pp. 109-110.

moved until the divine Name had, so to speak, vanished.

But the prophets had announced the coming of new times, the Messianic times when every man would be allowed to approach God and pray to him confidently. *"For then I will change and purify the lips of the peoples, that they all may call upon the name of the Lord"* (Zp 3:9).

And indeed Jesus Christ said to his disciples, *"This is how you are to pray: 'Our Father in heaven . . .' "* (Mt 6:9). St. Paul comments:

> *"You did not receive a spirit of slavery leading you back into fear, but a spirit of adoption through which we cry out, 'Abba!' (that is, 'Father')"* (Rm 8:15). *"The proof that you are sons is the fact that God has sent forth into our hearts the spirit of his Son which cries out 'Abba!' ('Father!') You are no longer a slave but a son!"* (Gal 4:6-7).

Henceforth Christians, without abandoning the reverential attitude which is at the heart of all religion, can "come close" to their God with affectionate trust, for they have learned that he is their Father. Let us listen to St. John: *"Beloved, if our consciences have nothing to charge us with, we can be sure . . . that we will receive at his hands whatever we ask"* (1 Jn 3:21-22). And once more, St. Paul: *"In Christ and through faith in him we can speak freely to God, drawing near to him with confidence"* (Ep 3:12).

Scripture refers to this bold filial assurance as the "(right to) say everything." The liturgy of every Mass invites us to it before the recitation of the Lord's Prayer: "Jesus taught us to call God our Father, and so we have the *courage* to say: . . ."

To win you over to the practice of this virtue, do I need to supplement these reflections with a contagious example? I shall cite St. Teresa of Avila. Burdened with difficult tasks, overcome with worry, she was moreover deprived of the sense of the presence of her God during mental prayer. Unable to stand it any more, she complained to the Lord one day, with as much filial boldness as respect:

* * *

"O my God, is it not enough that you hold me fast in this miserable life? That for love of You I accept this trial, and consent to remain in this exile in which everything conspires to keep me from possessing you, in which I must concern myself about eating and sleeping, about responsibilities, about my relations with a multitude of people?

"Nevertheless, I am resigned to everything for love of you! For you know very well, O my God, that it is an unspeakable torment for me! And now during the few moments left to me to enjoy your presence, you hide yourself from me! How can that be compatible with your mercy? How can your love for me tolerate it?

"Lord, if it were possible for me to hide from you the way you hide from me, I believe, indeed I am convinced, that your love for me would not tolerate it! But you see me always. Such inequality is too harsh, O my God. I beseech you, understand that it wrongs the one who loves you so much."

20. "Abba, Father!"

I n a recent letter, as you remember, I was searching for the essential element of mental prayer. Having determined that this essential element could not be the role assumed by the body, the intellect, or the emotions in prayer, I concluded that it lies in the will. That's true and it's also false. I am therefore writing to you again, to avoid misleading you.

It's true, in the sense that the person who prays can do nothing more or better than this act of the will, by which he or she turns toward God and surrenders to him. But the Christian's prayer is not only a human act. It is, first of all, an act on God's part. Obviously, God's intervention is more important than man's. This was implicit in my thinking as I wrote to you. Was it likewise implicit in your mind as you read the letter?

A poignant Biblical scene illustrates, in a very compelling way, what happens in Christian prayer. Manoah and his wife, after being visited by an angel of Yahweh, offered a sacrifice to the Lord in the angel's presence, on the altar in the fields (cf. Jg 13:19-20). They piled up the wood, set the kid on it, and lit the fire. Suddenly, the angel was as though sucked into the flames, and rose from earth to heaven.

A mysterious Being raises up the Christian's prayer, guides it, and carries it to the Father Almighty. This being is the Holy Spirit. St. Paul explains this wonderful teaching in the most explicit terms: *"The Spirit too helps us in our weakness, for we do not know how to pray as we ought; but the*

Spirit himself makes intercession for us with groanings that cannot be expressed in speech" (Rm 8:26).

This prayer of the Spirit within us makes our mental prayer so astonishingly great. We come to prayer tired in heart and mind, stammering trite things. No matter! From this dead wood, the Spirit brings forth a living flame.

It is impossible to grasp this prayer of the Spirit. And yet one word is understandable: *Abba*, Father. St. Paul tells us: *"Because you are sons, God has sent the Spirit of his Son into your hearts, who cries out: 'Abba, Father' "* (cf. Gal 4:6). The substance of our prayer is the Son's burst of filial love for his Father, which the Holy Spirit inspires in our souls. Why, then, should we be surprised that our human prayer is pleasing to God?

So long as we are still apprentices in the realm of mental prayer, we are not habitually conscious of this prayer of the Holy Spirit. We do not hear his cry of 'Father! Father!', although it resounds in the depths of our soul. Our interior senses, still poorly trained, are unaware of this presence in the Spirit within us. But from time to time, with deep inner joy (and with increasing frequency as our spiritual sense become more refined), we have a presentiment of the throbbing life of the Spirit of Christ. *"The Spirit himself gives witness with our spirit that we are children of God"* (Rm 8:16).

Understand this to mean that we discover within ourselves a burst of love for the Father, which we admit does not come from us. Prayer then is very simple. It consists in *consenting*, in *adhering* (two words filled with meaning for spiritual persons), to what is happening within us. It is simply a matter of surrendering ourselves to the prayer of the Holy Spirit, the way the oil in a lamp surrenders to the flame that sucks it in.

Very often, nothing reveals to us the mysterious activity of the Spirit. We must nonetheless consent and adhere to it. But we must do so in pure faith, and by that act of the will discussed in my last letter to you.

I cannot recommend this too highly to you. As you begin your mental prayer, make an explicit and vigorous act of faith in the Spirit of Christ, who wants to pray within you. And just as one signs a blank check, give him your anticipated and unreserved agreement.

"Blessed are the Poor" (Mt 5:3)

To come before the God of mercies, aware of one's sinfulness and deep-rooted poverty, and at the same time with the assurance of God's indefectible and generous tenderness—such is the fundamental attitude needed for mental prayer.

Mental prayer is a privileged moment for taking cognizance of our spiritual misery, and for offering ourselves to the embrace of divine mercy.

21 *The mental prayer of the sinner*—Sometimes it is the freedom that has lost the strength to resist the evil enticing it.

22 *The woolen yarn*—Once sin has been acknowledged, confessed, and rejected, it becomes poverty entrusted to God's gentle pity.

23 *"As for me, I know my sin"* (cf. Ps 51:5)—The Father's forgiveness calls into being a brand-new love within the soul's impurity and darkness.

24 *To someone who believes he is unworthy of praying*—The sin that is confessed cannot be an obstacle to encountering God. The sin that we refuse to acknowledge, especially our failure to love others, makes our mental prayer sterile.

25 *From head to foot*—But the feeling of total impotence during mental prayer is not necessarily the effect of sin. The Lord may permit it in order to inculcate in us the conviction that, in the realm of the spiritual, we are the poorest of the poor. To deploy one's poverty before God's eyes, is to pray.

26 *The mental prayer of poverty*—Anyone who is in the habit of knowing, willing, and doing things, finds it bitter to be reduced to indigence and impotence. It can be as fruitful as it is bitter: he learns to go from "I want" to "I beg you."

27 *Declaring bankruptcy*—Sin, impotence, and poverty make us discover our dependence on God. But anyone who loves, experiences dependence not as a servitude, but far more as a demand of his love.

28   *Dependence*—This dependence on the Lord is not accidental. It is congenital, radical, and total. To recognize it, to consent to it without reservation, that is giving oneself to God. Then the bond of dependence is converted into a bond of love.

29   *The watermark.*

21. The mental prayer of the sinner

I shall not deny that your letter deeply disturbed me. You wrote that, in my discussion of mental prayer, I seem to forget sinners. And you added: "No doubt because you do not deem them worthy of practicing it." May God preserve me from such pharisaism! Speaking as a sinner to his fellow sinners, to invite them to the act of conversion that is mental prayer. I am thinking only of them!

In any event, I reflected on my way of presenting mental prayer. It seems that in order to avoid the misunderstanding which you echoed, I should refer more often to that extraordinary page in St. Luke, the parable of "the prodigal son." Tortured by hunger, one day the poor fellow said to himself, *"I shall return to my father."* And the father, who went every day to the spot where he could look down the road, caught sight of him in the distance. *"He ran out to meet him, threw his arms around his neck, and kissed him"* (Lk 15:20).

Now, that's what mental prayer is: the privileged moment to become aware of our misery, and leave it behind by turning toward God. It is the meeting place between the Father and the child; the embrace of mercy with misery; the joyous feast of the prodigal's return.

Try to understand. It is not the child who purifies and sanctifies himself, and then comes to his father. Rather, he approaches in his impurity, clothed in repulsive rags. It is the paternal forgiveness that purifies him, transforms him, and clothes him in the festive garment. To speak plainly, without imagery, God, not man, purifies and sanctifies the sinner.

"A clean heart create for me, O God" (Ps 51:12). It is a gift of God, a freely-given gift that man cannot merit. It is granted to him if he dares to believe in it. What counts in the eyes of the Lord is that man should have a lofty idea of his God, and not hesitate to believe in mercy. What is so serious in the Lord's eyes is precisely that the elder son is scandalized by mercy, and sees it only as a lack of dignity, an insult to justice.

The race of the pharisees will never be able to understand. For them, it is man who sanctifies himself by his own efforts and moral feats. He then presents himself to God, worthy—as he now imagines—of talking with him, of being his intimate friend.

On the contrary, in the assembly of the saints, *"there will . . . be more joy in heaven over one repentant sinner than over ninety-nine righteous people who have no need to repent"* (Lk 15:7). The saints are filled with wonder at the spectacle of the mercy that gushes from the heart of God, every time a sinner comes before him who trusts and dares to believe in *"God's folly"* (1 Cor 1:25).

The sinner's prayer consists in bringing his misery to God, so that mercy may submerge it. It is indeed the prayer of each and all of us. As St. John affirms, *"If we say, 'We are free of the guilt of sin,' we deceive ourselves; the truth is not to be found in us"* (1 Jn 1:8; cf. 1 Jn 1:6, 10, 2:4, 4:20).

22. The woolen yarn

There is a short sentence in your letter, dear friend, that I cannot let pass unanswered: "I no longer have the right to pray." There is no situation that gives anyone the right to speak in this way. No one is ever deprived of the right to cry out to his God. It does not matter how sinful or degraded a man may be, even if he has lost his citizenship or been excommunicated from the Church. As long as he still has a breath of life in him, nobody can deny him the right to pray.

You add, "How could I speak to God, since I do not have the courage to make the break that would restore me to his friendship?"

In spite of these scarcely noble sentiments, you must praise the Lord for his perfections and for his admirable works. You must recognize his sovereignty by adoration, even if on one point you are denying it in practice. You must ask, even if you are not doing his will, that his kingdom come, and you must pray for others.

Why don't you take one more step that will bring you closer to his restored friendship? You do not have the strength to perform the act that he expects of you? So be it! But why not ask him for this strength? Perhaps you will answer, "I don't want him to give it to me." Then beg him to give you the desire to ask him for this strength. Again, you may say, as a good man said one day, "Really, the Lord is not proud!" That is certainly true.

We are the proud ones. We find it humiliating to be forced to "ask for the desire" to be healed of our evil. A poor prayer it is! And yet, it is already a living bond between man and God. If you are willing to offer this prayer, it will obtain the desire for you, and this will lead to your request. And after the request, strength will come to you, and it will bring about the break. Then, thanks to the break and God's forgiveness, your friendship with him will live again.

Allow me to put my lesson in the form of an anecdote, so that you cannot forget it.

* * *

The scene is a small British city in the 19th century. The large chimney for a factory has just been completed after many months of work. The last workman has come down from the top of the chimney, by way of the wooden scaffolding. The whole population of the town is there to celebrate the event, and first of all to witness the collapse of the large scaffolding.

Scarcely had the scaffolding come crashing down amid laughter and shouts when, to everyone's amazement, a worker appeared atop the chimney. He had been putting the final touches on some masonry inside the chimney. The spectators were filled with terror. It would take many days to set up new scaffolding, and by then the workman would be dead from the cold, if not from hunger. His aged mother was in tears.

But then, all of a sudden, she came out of the crowd, made a sign to her son, and shouted to him, "John! Take off your sock." Everyone was distressed. The poor woman had lost her mind! She insisted. So as not to grieve her, John obeyed. Then, she shouted, "Pull hard on the woolen yarn." He obeyed, and soon had an enormous handful of woolen yarn in his hands. "Now, throw one end of the yarn out, and hold the other end tightly in your fingers."

A flaxen thread was tied to the woolen yarn, and by pulling on the woolen yarn the young man brought the flaxen thread up to him. A piece of twine was tied to the flaxen thread, and then a rope was tied to the twine, and a cable to the rope. All John needed to do now, was to tie the cable more firmly and come down amid the cheers of the crowd.

* * *

Have I succeeded in convincing you to throw out a woolen thread to God? I hope so. I ask this of the Lord, with all my friendship for you.

23. *"As for me, I know my sin"* (cf. Ps 51:5)

I have taken advantage of the vacation season to come to a town in the provinces, to visit a very elderly priest whom I venerate. He is paralyzed and no longer leaves his room. From his armchair he looks out on the apse of his former cathedral, and he prays unceasingly.

It is hard for me to define the feeling I experience in his presence. It is as if an extraordinary purity emanated from him, and imbued those around him. It is a purity that emanates from him, but does not originate in him: the shining forth of the Purity of God, through a person who has become diaphanous. As I listened to him, I wondered how he had attained this transparence. One word forced itself on me: humility. As a matter of fact, he often alluded to his "misery" with a very noticeable accent of peaceful, trusting, and joyful suffering.

Your letter had just reached me, in which you say, "I prefer not to think too much about my sins." Your words came to my mind during our conversation, contrasting curiously with the attitude of my interlocutor. I cited them to him, without naming you, of course. As a result, I was favored with the following very precious remarks.

* * *

"Look at the publican in the parable. There he is before God, not daring to raise his eyes. He beats his breast, he does not stop repeating: 'God, forgive the sinner that I am.' He is wonderfully humble. But in his case humility is not, as it is in many people, just one more virtue of which to be quite proud. In a simple way, he is expressing to God what he realizes about himself all through the day: that he is a sinner.

'In a sense, that is all the Lord expects from us in order to lavish his gifts on us: knowledge, avowal, rejection of sin, and sorrow for it. Like St. Paul, I speak of sin in the singular, of the evil within us from which our many sins flow. It is impossible to get rid of sin. It sticks to the soul.

"But we can do better than to grieve and despair. We can do better than to simply hide from God, the way Adam did after his sin, or than to ask God to leave us, the way Peter did after the miraculous draught of fish. We can present ourselves to the Lord in our naked truth, and show him our wounds. Sin that is discerned, avowed, and repudiated, is no longer sin but only 'misery,' and calls down God's most gentle mercy upon us.

"Because we acknowledge our sin, call it by its right name, dissociate ourselves from it, and expose it to God's purifying gaze, suddenly it is no longer pernicious, and we are miraculously purified. The man who, during prayer and through the day, lives in this attitude of confessing his sin to God, is a limpid pool in which the purity of heaven is reflected."

                              * * *

During our conversation, I let the following exclamation slip out: "Ah! I really know this old self of mine, swarming with sin!" The reply came so quickly that I thought for an instant that my friend was delivered from his paralysis.

                              * * *

"Do not calumniate *the depths of your being.* In a child of God, it is not the innermost being that is contaminated by sin, but only certain obscure regions that have not yet been evangelized. Never forget that the innermost being of a Christian, after his baptism, is luminous, radiant, and infinitely pure, thanks to the presence within it of the Blessed Trinity. If Christians only understood that heaven is not somewhere else, but right there within them, in the heart of their heart. Their innermost self is already completely immersed in the infinite love of God. If they realized it, they would need to do only one thing: allow this love to destroy the last pockets of resistance, and conquer all the cantons of their interior world!"

                              * * *

Are you going to say that I am not really answering your request for advice on the way to proceed with your mental prayer? But this attitude of avowing our sin is the warp and woof of all true prayer, as indeed it is of the Christian life.

24. To someone who believes he is unworthy of praying

I was questioning a widow on the development of her spiritual life, so as to counsel her in a more knowledgeable way. She told me:

* * *

"I owe my interior life to Sergius [her husband]. More precisely, to his attitude toward me during a shameful phase of my conjugal life. Married for five years and the mother of two children, I was being unfaithful to him. But I still loved him. Not wanting to destroy his happiness, I made sure that he had no reason to suspect me.

"His love for me, of exceptional quality, deepened day after day. One evening—I remember it as if it were yesterday—he expressed his tenderness, his esteem, and his admiration for me in terms that touched my heart. It was too much. The words escaped me: 'If you only knew!' He answered, 'I do know.' These words triggered violent indignation on my part, unjustified as it was.

" 'Well then, why are you playing this shocking game with me? Either you are not hurt by what you know—and that is proof that you do not love me—or else you are greatly disturbed and your serenity is only a lie!'

"I was beside myself—aggressive, scoffing, insulting. He waited until the storm was over. Then he replied calmly, gravely, tenderly: 'Please understand! For six months I have been suffering cruelly. My own suffering was bearable, because it didn't degrade me. But your evil did degrade you, and this was intolerable for my love. I saw clearly what I had to do, the only thing I could do. I had to love you still more than before, so that you might be resurrected to love, that this brand-new love might not only burn away your evil in its flames, but create a new heart for you, a new purity, a more radiant beauty than ever.' And in fact Sergius' love made me into this new being right then and there."

* * *

This woman's disclosure enabled me to grasp more clearly what true forgiveness is. When forgiveness is condescending, it begets revolt. When it is reticent, it is burdensome. Forgiveness without love can neither deliver nor save. Only true forgiveness, the fruit of a very pure love, can call forth a living wellspring in the heart of the unfaithful one. Only that can regenerate the one who betrayed love, by enabling him or her to be reborn to love.

Can I hope that recounting this distant memory will help you to understand what God is expecting of you? You wrote: "I feel I am unworthy of praying." Well then, when will you pray? When you have succeeded in extricating yourself from sin, in stripping yourself of every stain and imperfection? Are you going to forget that only the love of Christ can purify you, transform you, and sanctify you?

Instead of fleeing from Christ, why don't you pray mentally and expose your sinner's soul to his gaze? You will discover that for God, to forgive is to love. It is so intense, that a brand-new love springs up within the darkness and impurity of the soul, a love that not only purifies and regenerates it, but makes it accede to a totally new perfection.

Think of the look that Christ gave Peter, who had just denied him. Do you believe that it was a look of reproach or anger? Far more terrible, it was a look of more intense love, expressing a more solicitous, burning, and encompassing tenderness than ever. Peter could not resist it. His heart was broken, pouring itself out in tears that were at once bitter and sweet.

At the same time, under the conjoined action of Christ's gaze and of his Spirit at work in Peter, a new love took possession of his whole being. As a result, just a few days after his denial, he dared to affirm to Christ without hesitation: "You know well that I *love you*" (Jn 21:17). He could have added, "I have loved you in very truth since the other night." Peter was not lying. This new love, that his Master's gaze had caused to well up in him, would impel him onward until he gave his own life on a cross, after a life consumed in preaching to the multitudes about the way that God loves us.

25. *From head to foot*

A number of things make you unhappy and anxious: your meditations as arid as a desert, your lack of spiritual vitality at the hour of prayer, the feeling that the Lord no longer opens the door at which you are constantly knocking. You tell me that you are eager to rediscover, if not fervor, at least those periods of mental prayer in which you were sure that you were not wasting your time. I certainly have no infallible advice to give you. I would simply invite you to find out for yourself what God is expecting of you.

It is possible that this is a trial permitted by the Lord to whet your desire, and stimulate your search and your trust. But it may also be a signal, a warning that something is lacking in your life. I ask you not to eliminate the latter hypothesis too quickly.

You write: "Never before have I striven so scrupulously to follow your advice on the practice of mental prayer." I am the first to agree. That is precisely what makes me think that there is something in need of change, not so much in your manner of praying as in your life.

In the Christian life, everything is interrelated. If the practice of one virtue is neglected, if the sacraments are not received often enough, and if the will of God is disregarded on some point, the effects are felt everywhere, and first of all in the life of prayer. That is why I am not sure that your intense effort to pray better is the best course for you. Begin by trying to discover whether God is expecting some reform on your part.

Examine yourself first on the theological life, the foundation of the Christian life. And in the very first place, examine yourself on charity. Perhaps you are not gracious to your neighbor, eager to serve him, to witness to the love of God, who has given you an insight into and a taste for his infinite goodness. That would explain why the Lord—I will not say rejects you, but—withdraws from you the sense of his presence and of his love.

Love those around you. Make an effort to reach out to those with whom you are less spontaneously sympathetic. Ask yourself whether there are certain persons who are expecting, in vain, some material or moral help from you. It is very possible that progress in charity will enable you to recover the reassuring presence of God in your mental prayer, or at least the sense of not wasting your time at it. Christ cannot resist the prayers of those who, for their part, do not resist the appeals of their neighbors. As you well know, he considers whatever we do to others as being done to himself. St. Augustine, in his commentary on the First Epistle of St. John, identifies Christ with his members by means of an unexpected and vigorous comparison, impossible to forget:

* * *

"He whom you adore in his head, you outrage in his body. He, for his part, loves his body. If you remove yourself from the body, the Head does not cut itself off from its body. From heaven, the Head cries out, 'It is in vain that you honor me, it is in vain that you honor me.' It is as if someone wanted to kiss your head by walking on your feet. His heavy hobnailed shoes would crush your feet while he was trying to grasp your head in his hands to kiss it. Would you not interrupt these demonstrations of respect with a scream and say: 'What are you doing, wretched one, you are crushing me!' You would not say, 'You are crushing my head,' since he is honoring the head. But the head would speak louder for the members that are being crushed than for the honors it is receiving.

"The head would cry out, 'I want none of your honors. Stop crushing me!' If you answer, 'How can you say that I am crushing you? On the contrary, I want to give you a kiss, I want to embrace you.' 'But don't you see, foolish one, that, by virtue of the oneness that makes the body one single entity, what you want to embrace is present in what you are crushing? You honor me above, but you crush me below. There is greater suffering in what you are crushing than there is joy in what you are honoring, because what you honor suffers for the member you are crushing.' "

* * *

I would be inclined to interpret this astonishing page in this way: "You come to mental prayer to kiss my face, but you refuse your brother the honor and help he expects from you—and that I expect from you in him. Do not be surprised, therefore, that I react to you like a man who pulls away from someone who is stepping on his feet."

I do not claim to have infallibly expressed Christ's sentiments toward you. I simply invite you to ask yourself a question.

26. *The mental prayer of poverty*

S hall I dare tell you that I am delighted over the sense of total impotence and failure you experience in your mental prayer? Believe me, it is not hardness of heart on my part, but the conviction that this harsh trial holds great benefits for you.

You have abundant intellectual and material resources. You hold a position of authority. You are admired and feared, loved and obeyed. Many people and many things depend on you. And yet here is one area, the area of mental prayer, in which you are failing. You have made intense efforts to succeed, but to no avail. And you inform me in your letter that mental prayer is not for you, that you are giving it up.

I beg of you, agree to think it over some more before giving it up. This daily time of prayer seems intolerable to you. Does the cause lie perhaps in your secret refusal to admit that you can be indigent, powerless, and poor, even for a half hour a day? If you have no sooner begun your mental prayer, than you feel the urge to return to your professional activities, is it not because you are driven to prove to others (and first of all to yourself) that you are a "capable" man, creative and efficient? Be on your guard. I fear that you are yielding to an insidious, dangerous temptation, that threatens to throw you into the company of those whom Christ condemned: the rich. A rich man is a "somebody" who *can*, who *has*, and who *is*.

You need mental prayer so very much! In your current life, dominated by success, mental prayer offers you the opportunity to discover your limitations, to experience the truest, most beneficial poverty, poverty of soul. Bless it for enabling you to rediscover your childhood, the time when you could not do much of anything, didn't possess anything, and, tiny and weak, were dependent upon others for everything. In the Kingdom of God, everyone is a child, defenseless, destitute, and poor.

You ought to read more of the Bible to discover the Beatitude of the poor, and meditate on it. I am not speaking only of the few lines in the Gospel, known as the Beatitudes. The whole of the Bible is the Beatitude of the poor. From beginning to end, it sings their praises.

But we need to understand what we mean by these words "poverty" and "poor." Their definition is to be found not in the dictionary, but in the sacred texts.

In the most ancient Scriptural texts, the Hebrew words designating the poor are concrete terms: "beggar," "puny one," "cripple." They express the physical attitude of the poor. Over the centuries, these words gradually took on religious meaning. They came to express an attitude of soul, rather than a physical or sociological reality. The person who humbly seeks God, turns to him, and fears and serves him, has been called the poor man. It is easy to see how, over the years, there has been a shift from one meaning to the other. Quite naturally, the Jew who had no money or work, who did not eat his fill, whom the powerful persecuted, turned to God since he could obtain no help from men.

Finally, during the last centuries before Jesus Christ, the poor, the *"anawim,"* were the devout Jews whether or not they were deprived of material possessions. Besides, the name "poor" suited them. They, too, were in need, and were hungry and thirsty. They hungered and thirsted for "the consolation of Israel," for God. It is to them that Christ spoke on the mountain: *"Blessed are the poor in spirit . . . the afflicted . . . those who hunger . . ."* (cf. Mt. 5:3-12). The most blessed one of all was Mary, because she was perfectly poor.

Now do you understand why you need mental prayer? For a half hour a day, it makes you a poor man. Choose to be blessed! Do you see why I say that your ineptness at mental prayer is a benefit? It helps you to discover and accept, not only your inability to pray, but even more fundamentally, your inability to save yourself by your own means. It forces you to adopt the attitude of a beggar, who trusts that everything will be given to him freely by God's inexhaustible love. Please persevere. Gradually, peace will replace your exasperation, and you will find that you can remain at the Lord's feet, happy to be poor. You will at last have discovered that to pray is to lay one's poverty before the eyes of God.

When you feel the need, make use of the prayers of the "poor" (often called "little ones," "the lowly," "the oppressed," "the miserable ones") that have been preserved for us in the Psalter.

27. Declaring bankruptcy

Do you know what I was thinking, as I read your last letter? That you are acting like a business executive even in your life of mental prayer. Believe me, I do not scorn the businessman that you are.

Rather, I have a secret admiration for the human gifts which make up your strength and your success: initiative, clarity of vision, the will to succeed, a sense of organization and command, and efficiency.

But mental prayer is not a human affair, and the mentality of the businessman has no place in it. Now, I believe I glimpse signs of this mentality in your reactions. During our first encounter, you asked me to suggest subjects for mental prayer, and you were disappointed when I told you that I knew of none better than the Gospels. You answered, "Reading the Gospel doesn't help me very much to pray." In your letter, you complain that you cannot find a precise method of mental prayer in our *Cahiers*. This seems to reveal your "business executive" mentality, concerned with efficiency, productivity, and profits.

Far be it from me to think or say anything against the ancient instinct to succeed that is embedded deep within our being. Mankind owes its development and progress to it. The evils associated with the desire to succeed are caused, not by it, but by its perversion by egotism, ambition, and the will to power. But this instinct to succeed is the worst possible obstacle to prayer. Mental prayer is not a human undertaking, to be successfully executed. It is a willingness to give in. That is perhaps why you find it so difficult. In your eyes, to abdicate is the worst cowardice. After all, isn't a difficulty meant to be mastered and opposition meant to be overcome? You are probably right where business is concerned, but not in the realm of prayer.

You are engaged in mental prayer. You question a page of the Gospel, and it does not answer. You knock, and the door remains closed. That is enough to exasperate you. It is not one of your habits to accept resistance on the part of men and things. And besides, you reflect, what good is it to dawdle, to lose precious time that could be used more effectively, perhaps even in God's service? Or else you say, "Let someone else find an efficient method!"

Well no, you must accept the resistance of that page which withholds its secrets from you. It is not a question of seeking another, more eloquent page, or taking up a more stimulating book of spirituality, or of discovering an infallible method of meditation. You need: to confess that you are powerless to understand God's thoughts; to humiliate yourself in the presence of this mute text; to prostrate yourself before God's silent transcendence. You need to wait in the attitude of the repentant sinner until the Lord deigns to have pity, and grants you the grace of prayer. You have no right at all to this grace. God will give it to you freely in his own time.

Grace is freely given, and is not capricious. If it is slow in coming, it is not that God hesitates to give. It is because you are slow to clear the paths by which the Lord wants to take possession of your being.

A memory comes to mind whose meaning you should grasp better than anyone. A friend of mine was about to declare the bankruptcy of his business. His wife came to see me one day, greatly disturbed. She could not understand her husband's reaction to this situation, which she described to me:

* * *

"I cannot find words to translate what is going on inside of him: suffering, collapse—words such as these do not apply. It is much more than suffering, and it is not collapse, since he is reacting and doing everything that the situation demands. It is a kind of death, as if he had been stricken in the wellsprings of his life, in his dignity as a man. It seems that we women are incapable of imagining the interior disaster that failure means to a man when it affects his undertakings, his creative activity. We experience such distress only at the level of love."

* * *

I am sure that you evaluate better than my visitor this dismay of a man confronting bankruptcy. Might not your revulsion against mental prayer be of the same nature? In the mainstream of your life you are a success, but here you are a failure. Everywhere else you are called upon to combat, but here you are required to abdicate, to declare bankruptcy. That goes counter to all your habits, and more than that, counter to the essential aspirations of your being. You love to conquer, and you are right in feeling that way. But please understand that where God is concerned our victory is to consent to be conquered. Consider St. Paul on the road to Damascus.

In your daily activities, you say, "I want." At mental prayer, you must say, "I beg of you." There you are no longer the man who wields authority, but the child who asks, the beggar who holds out his hand, the failure who accepts humiliation.

To succeed in life we need to know, to will, and to have the power to do. To succeed in mental prayer you need to agree to know nothing, will nothing, and have power to do nothing, so that God may give you his knowledge, his will, and his power.

Some time ago you said to me, "That's contrary to nature!" Yes, I can readily see that it is torture for you (for you more than for someone else) to remain there powerless before God. I can understand that you would prefer any activity at all, indeed, any other kind of torture but this. But it is precisely through mental prayer that this turning around of your nature will come about, this conversion that is the only way of adapting yourself to God's action.

On the other hand, don't imagine that I am inviting you to a quietistic passivity. To abdicate, to declare bankruptcy at the hour of mental prayer, is a very positive act. It implies intense spiritual activity. It presupposes that you believe in God present and acting, that you are mercilessly mortifying everything in you that clamors to live and to succeed. It presupposes that you are giving yourself (or rather are waiting patiently), in an attitude of offering and receptiveness, for God to come and take possession of you.

28. Dependence

First of all, here is the principal passage of a letter I have just received:

***

"I am forty years old and I've never been sick until now. This is an entirely new experience for me, and I assure you, not a pleasant one. During the first days, revolt rumbled within me. There I was, passing from hand to hand like a lost-and-found object being wantonly handled, and without anyone's even deigning to give a serious answer to my demands for explanations.

"And to think that in my daily life I cannot tolerate to have my secretary move even my paper-cutter on my desk! What a horrible feeling of being nothing more than a *thing*. Certainly, a thing that is being taken care of, examined, repaired, and whose proper functioning is being checked out, but nevertheless a thing, that is to say, a passive, inanimate being. I thought with envy of the most miserable hobo. Anyone who disposes of himself freely is a great lord by comparison with this middle-class businessman in a comfortable hospital who has become a thing controlled by others."

* * *

I want to tell you what went through my mind when I read these lines. This will be a continuation of our last conversation.

My correspondent is right. There is nothing more intolerable for a free man, legitimately proud of his self-determination, than to become dependent on others. That means losing his dignity as a human person. But the truth is that independence is of the spiritual order. In a hospital, in a concentration camp, amid tortures, men and women can remain free. Their bodies are the prey of others, but their souls can escape capture. It is only when man abdicates that he becomes a thing. I acknowledge, nonetheless, that physical dependence is a restriction to man's independence. That is the first reason why it appears intolerable to him.

Well now, this independence is what a lover feels, an irrepressible need to sacrifice to the one he loves, precisely because it is his most precious possession. To sacrifice this possession is the irrefutable proof that he loves the other more than himself.

To pray is to transpose these sentiments into our relations with God. It is to be happy and proud to be God's property. It is to repose in a dependence that is accepted, willed, and loved. The man of prayer cherishes this dependence the more that he discovers it to be radical and innate. He has the power to revolt against it, but he cannot change the fact that he is indebted to God for his very existence—not just once and for all, but at every moment of his life.

Mental prayer is the time when, driving off the illusion of autonomy, man becomes aware again of his fundamental dependence. It is the time when he consents to this dependence, and places himself once more into the Father's hands to be disposed of as God wills. *"In manus tuas, Domine. . . ."* "Into your hands, Lord, I commend my spirit."

There was an old priest who understood this very well. His entire spiritual life gravitated around the idea of his dependence vis-a-vis God. One day he confided to me, "I need only think of the word 'dependence' to be deep in mental prayer."

29. The watermark

A fter writing you that one of the fundamental attitudes of mental prayer is to offer oneself to the Lord, I have had second thoughts. Am I perhaps leading you into an error so common that it is surprising that anyone has escaped it?

Each of us likes to believe he is his own master—autonomous and free. And we think the most beautiful act is precisely to renounce our independence, to proclaim our dependence upon God by giving ourselves to him. Some of us are even close to thinking that the Lord really owes us something in exchange for this gift—a certain esteem and gratitude.

It is true that there is nothing nobler than for a free person to agree to depend on another through love. Such, for example, is the case of a bride on her wedding day. But it is not true that we are our own masters in our relations with God.

Hold a piece of bond paper up to the light, and you will read the name of the manufacturer in the watermark. Look at a man in the light of God, and you will discover the name of his Lord inscribed in the very fabric of his being.

Man is made by God and belongs to him the same way a crop belongs to a farmer, or a sculpture to an artist. And not merely "the same way," but much more so. Things belong to a man because they are the fruit of his labors, but they do not owe their total being to him. He did not create them. Man receives everything from God. He therefore belongs to God far more completely. He belongs to God totally, definitively, and exclusively. Everything in man belongs to God: his intellect and heart, his body and soul, his actions and possessions. Whether he knows it or not, whether he consents to it or not, the reality of his origin remains. He comes from God, and he belongs to God. This dependence does not result from any self-giving on his part.

What, then, do we mean by "giving oneself" to God? Certainly, not what these words mean in our human relations. With God, to give oneself is to recognize the irrefutable, indisputable, "non-modifiable" fact that we all belong to him. It is to acknowledge it with our intellect, consent to it with all our heart, and ratify it with all the fervor of our will. In this way, an essential change comes about in us. The bond of dependence is transformed into a bond of love.

The damned belong to God no less than do the saints. This dependence makes the happiness of the saints, because they accept it. It tortures the damned because they obstinately persist in rejecting it. For the saint, it is a communion of love, for the damned it is hell. But for both the saint and the damned, it *is*.

When you pray, make sure you avoid the naive and pretentious attitude of the person who wants to *become* dependent upon God through a glorious gift of himself. Rather, realize that you already belong to God, down to the innermost fibers of your being. This attitude will give you a deep and humble joy, a sense of total security. When you experience it, consent to this belonging to God with your whole heart, your whole soul, and your whole mind. That is giving yourself to God.

"Eternal life is this: to know you . . ." (Jn 17:3)

Knowledge plays a primordial role in our relations with God, as it does in love. This is particularly true in mental prayer. We need to know in order to love, and to know better in order to love better.

Knowledge of God arouses love of God. Love, to use the words of St. Augustine, "yearns for the holy leisure of mental prayer," where it is renewed and strengthened through a better knowledge of the Lord.

30 *Time stolen from God*—Assiduous meditation on God's perfections brings forth in us the great fundamental attitudes of prayer: adoration, praise, reverent fear, thanksgiving, self-offering.

31 *Reacting to God*—Our supernatural faculty to know is faith. Since it is often dormant, it is important to awaken it, and exercise and develop it through meditation and mental prayer. It then becomes eagerness to know the living God.

32 *Knowing in order to love*—God speaks to us in many ways in order to make himself known. His works reveal him, and first among all these works is marriage, in which divine love is reflected.

33 *Letter to Paul and Monique*—Reflection on the great joys that govern the conjugal life makes possible a better understanding of the demands and riches of the life of mental prayer, which is also an encounter, a communion of love.

34 *To a young man engaged to be married*—God reveals himself by his words far more even than by his works. For lack of meditation on the Scriptures, our faith withers. Nourished by God's Word, faith bears abundant and delectable fruit.

35 *The arid garden*—God was not content to speak to us through his works and his spokesmen. To make himself known to us, he sent his

Son. "Listen to him" is the Father's command. We must listen attentively to him, with our whole mind, our whole heart, and our whole
being.

36   *"Listen to him"* (Mt 17:5)—Then, little by little, the knowledge of
the unfathomable riches of Christ will awaken our admiration and love,
and open up the wellsprings of our prayer.

37   *"The unfathomable riches of Christ"* (Ep 3:8)—Christ made this
essential revelation to us from the Cross. That is why we must never tire
of meditating on the book that is the Cross.

38   *The deepest book*—But we must still understand its language. It is
not a panegyric of suffering, but the proclamation of conquering love.

39   *Should we pray before the crucifix?*

30. Time stolen from God

How could anyone dare say to you: "The hours you spend in prayer
are hours stolen from God, because God is waiting for you in the
neighbor you neglect for the sake of mental prayer"? How can anyone
be so completely mistaken about the purpose of human life? And show
such scorn for people?

For people are scorned when they are seen to have only the right to
serve God as slaves—slaves forbidden to raise their eyes toward a
haughty master who would never dream of admitting them into his
close friendship.

You run your business with constant concern for social justice. The
best part of your leisure time is devoted to the organization you
founded to aid developing countries. Despite these responsibilities, you
are a husband and father who is very "present" to his family. And you
say it troubles your conscience that you reserve a half hour a day and
one Saturday morning a month for prayer and meditation on the Word
of God!

I beg of you, don't let unjust criticisms influence you. The "heresy of
action," of which Pius XII spoke on various occasions, has not
disappeared.

I could understand your scruples if nurturing your faith, meditation and prayer were a luxury, or at least a pastime like stamp-
collecting, bridge, or perhaps reading Montaigne, Saint-Simon, or
Voltaire. But for a Christian, seeking to know God better comes first.

You may object that love takes priority over knowledge. That's true, but knowledge and love go hand in hand. Progress in love is scarcely possible without a persevering "search for the face of God," to use the expression dear to the Psalmist. On the supernatural level, no less than on the purely human level, to know better leads to loving better, and loving better awakens the desire to know better.

Besides, God himself invited men to know him: *"Desist! and confess that I am God"* (Ps 46:11).

St. Thomas Aquinas explains: "It is of the nature of friendship to converse with one's friend. Now, the conversation of man with God is carried on through contemplation."

Interpret contemplation to be the effort (which you are making) to know God through spiritual reading and mental prayer. More precisely, it is the simple, penetrating, and delightful knowledge in which this effort normally culminates.

St. Augustine has left us a passage on this subject that will completely reassure you, I hope.

* * *

"Love of truth aspires to the holy leisure of mental prayer, but the demands of charity impel to honorable labors. When these labors are not required of us, there is nothing to hinder our search for truth and contemplation. If these labors are required, charity demands that we accomplish them. But even in such a case, it is important not to set the joy of contemplation completely aside, lest, deprived of this sweetness, we succumb at our task."

31. Reacting to God

In psychology as well as in biology, there is an in-depth study of *reactions*, defined as the responses of a living being to stimuli. I wonder why, in the area of spirituality, so little attention is paid to this notion. And yet, in one sense, we must say that the spiritual life—and prayer in particular—is man's reaction to God.

All the fundamental religious attitudes of the human person at prayer (adoration, self-offering, praise, fear, thanksgiving and consecration) are understandable only from this point of view.

Let us suppose the thought of God's transcendence comes to your mind, either suddenly as the effect of a grace, or perhaps at the end of a laborious meditation. Are you not irresistibly impelled to prostrate yourself like a Bedouin at the hour of prayer? To prostrate not only your body, but your mind, your heart and your whole life?

When you discover that everything comes from God, do you not experience the need to give your whole being back to God, in a surge of self-offering and submission?

When you see a reflection from God's splendor in creatures, does not admiration rise from your heart to your lips in a hymn of praise? Many of the Psalms were born of this contemplation!

When God allows you to glimpse his holiness, do you not experience a feeling of awe, a reverential fear, a quivering of your whole being, a keen awareness not only of your own smallness but also of your sinfulness? Isaiah, suddenly confronting the holiness of the Lord, cried out, *"Woe is me, I am doomed! For I am a man of unclean lips"* (Is 6:5).

When you remember the many graces you have received during your life, does not thanksgiving (that turning of the grateful creature toward the Creator, that joyous leap of the child toward his Father) completely elate you?

And if, one day, the infinite love with which you are loved reveals itself, do you not feel the need to consecrate yourself to God by offering him your whole being?

Now do you understand what I meant when I told you that prayer is the soul's reaction to God? Obviously, all these interior attitudes are not necessarily explicit in each and every hour of mental prayer. One or another of them predominates. But the religious roots of our prayer consist of these great sentiments that persevering mental prayer accumulates little by little.

It would be just as absurd to claim that we can draw these wellsprings of prayer from within ourselves, without first meditating on the perfections of God, as for a mirror to claim that it makes light emanate from itself.

Some day God may take the initiative in letting you glimpse one or another of his perfections. But in the meantime, you must set out to discover them gropingly and continue to meditate without getting discouraged, sustained by a joyful hope.

32. *Knowing in order to love*

I must say, your disdain for meditation does not appear totally pure to me. You are right in thinking that mental prayer is not supposed to be an intellectual exercise but a time of intimacy with God, and that the intellect must give precedence to the heart. But I fear that, under the pretext of saving the primacy of love, you underestimate the place mental prayer must give to knowledge of God.

Your attitude is one that women tend to espouse, whereas men are more inclined to intellectualism. Both tendencies are dangerous. Men must be warned of the peril they face. This is all the more formidable because their spiritual life is compartmentalized. They are not always making connections between their intellect, heart and will. Knowledge does not necessarily lead them to love. But the affective mental prayer that you rightly hold in esteem conceals another danger. A love inadequately nourished by knowledge can degenerate into sentimentalism.

It is not only women who tend to belittle and reject meditation, but your whole generation. It is probably a reaction against the methods of meditation that are accused of imprisoning the soul instead of giving it wings. It is nonetheless regrettable that the deserved discredit into which certain methods have fallen should extend to all efforts to know God.

Call to mind the conference you attended with your husband a month ago. I told you that marital love declines when spouses give up their daily search to discover each other. The same applies to our relations with God. Love is jeopardized when the effort to know him slackens. Knowledge and love (that is to say, faith and charity) are closely interrelated.

Refuse to resign yourself to a faith, to a knowledge of God, that is half-asleep. Awaken it. How? The way you get your little son Mark to wake up in the morning. He is slow to open his eyes, and his lids are heavy with sleep. He does not recognize anything around him, and goes back to sleep. Finally, after your repeated calls, he awakens and focuses his eyes on your face smiling at him. He smiles back and suddenly takes an interest in the beautiful day you promise him.

Do the same for your faith. Offer your faith something that will capture its attention. Draw it anew to the face of God, which it could no longer discern in its dormant state.

But it is not in a few moments (or even a few weeks) that one awakens a dormant faith, and gives it alacrity, penetration, and intense life. The great means of reviving faith, of enriching and vitalizing it, is mental prayer, that is, meditation. Persons whose faith is keenly alive, because they nurture it day after day by study and reflection, need only to love God when they go to mental prayer. They are prepared. For others, there is need of patient, laborious exercise in knowing God through the practice of mental prayer-meditation. In the end, their faith will certainly come awake and alive. It will arouse their love, and raise their hearts up in prayer.

I recommend that you recite the following prayer of St. Augustine from time to time. It will kindle in you the need to know and will stimulate your search.

* * *

"O Lord my God, my only hope, listen to me! Do not permit me to stop seeking you out of lassitude, but grant that I may eagerly seek your face. Give me the strength to seek you, just as you have enabled me to find you more and more. Here before you are my strength and my infirmity: guard my strength, heal my infirmity. Here before you are my knowledge and my ignorance: where you have opened the way to me, welcome my coming; where you have closed the door, open it to my cry."

33. Letter to Paul and Monique

You, too, are asking me for a book of meditations! You will have to learn to decipher the book that God has given you: your marriage.

Let me explain. When I was a young priest, I used to enjoy visiting a painter friend of mine in his studio. True artists have a quality of soul that seems to be their privilege (I do not say their monopoly, since this quality is also found in the saints). It is a certain freshness of feeling— perhaps I should call it candor—that is closely akin to spiritual childhood. My friend possessed this quality in a rare degree. The years had, as it were, filtered and purified this precious quality of soul in him. When he took his visitors around his studio, presenting his canvases to them, and marveling at them like a young mother before her newborn child, no one was annoyed. For there was no trace of vanity in his manner, only fervor.

Even more than his paintings, I loved to contemplate his beautiful, vibrant face. His astonishingly mobile features reflected different nuances and vibrations, depending on the canvas he was describing. He did not love all his works equally. He would linger with special predilection before some of them, no doubt the ones in which he had expressed the best that was in him. He delighted in them with a childlike joy, watching for my reaction. This joy intensified as I began to understand his canvas better (or rather his feelings, of which the canvas was simply the reflection).

Many a time, after leaving his studio, my thoughts turned to God. God, in the vast studio that is the universe, leads us by the hand to present his works to us. He wants to help us spell them out and to discover their deep inner meaning, so that he can introduce us through them to his own thoughts and sentiments. God is not engrossed by all of his creatures in the same degree. There are some before which he stops, and before which he makes us pause at greater length. They are the ones into which he has put the best of himself, through which he reveals his loftiest perfections to us. Love, the union of man and woman, is among them.

Everything had been created, one day after the other, and on the sixth day the creation of man had been the crowning achievement. However, God's divine endeavor was still unfinished. It still remained for marriage to be instituted. And so God formed Eve and united her to Adam. This union of man and woman spoke eloquently of his magnificent plan, still hidden in the mists of the future: the union between his Son and redeemed humanity. How could he not have a predilection for marriage, the last of his creations in point of time?

It is no surprise, therefore, that we are constantly making discoveries about life in the married state. No surprise that all the mystics, following the Bible, speak of marriage as a symbol of the riches of love that union with Christ holds for us. Paul and Monique, please understand that your married life is filled with meaning. Don't be like those illiterates who look at a written page and don't realize that it means something, that it is perhaps a beautiful poem.

Your marriage is not only a great human reality. It is also rich with supernatural meaning. There is Someone who reveals his heart to you

through marriage, who reveals his impatient desire to establish between each of you and himself bonds of love that will give far greater
happiness than those of marriage. There is Someone who, through
your marriage, wants to help you understand what he hopes from you,
what your relationship with him should be throughout life.

I want to cite three texts that will show you how we are to read and
understand the parable that is human love. I am correct in saying
"parable," because human love is written in a cipher. A certain "innocence of the eyes" is needed to decipher the divine message that lies
hidden within marriage.

The first text is in a letter from a friend who lives in Morocco. His
wife had spent her vacation in France, far from him, but was soon
expected home. He was preparing himself for her return. In so doing,
his thoughts rose to noble heights:

"I am expecting Francoise in a week. If we prepared for our Com-
munions the way we prepare to see our spouses again, I think we would
make serious progress in the knowledge and love of Christ."

I excerpt the second text from Jacques Maillet's *Lettres à sa fiancée*.
He was deeply convinced that divine love surpasses human love, without thereby lessening the value of the latter. His love for Madeleine
made him think of God, and his love of God made him think of
Madeleine.

* * *

"To think of you, Madeleine, is to be obliged to regain a more
naive joyousness, to be forced to combat sadness, so as to be
worthier of one of your glances. My attitude toward the one I love
teaches me the attitude I should have toward God. It gives me a
keener desire to be in his presence, to do his will which is never
capricious. It teaches me an interior recollection where his presence should eclipse all lesser concerns. If only I yearned for God
the way I yearn for my little Mad! If only I was as eager at every
moment to cast aside everything that separates me from God the
way I strive to remove every obstacle that furtively comes between
you and me!"

* * *

Last, there is this testimony cited among others in the report on the Inquiry on Mental Prayer published in a special issue of *L'Anneau d'Or*: "Seigneur, apprends-nous à prier" ("Lord, teach us to pray").

One woman recounts that she discovered the meaning of mental prayer from her dialogue with her husband. Does not this dialogue (which sometimes attains a superhuman quality in an atmosphere of silence) bear the same relation to human love, that mental prayer does to the union of the human person with God? Is it not the moment of intense intimacy, in which love expresses itself most perfectly and is at the same time renewed?

* * *

"Once I had decided to practice mental prayer, I simply "jumped in" without really knowing how to go about it. And then suddenly there was a light. . . . First and above all, I probably had to establish a state of spiritual intimacy between myself and God. After that, it was very simple, since I have been in training in that kind of "gymnastics" in my married life.

"When I want our evenings together to be times of true intimacy, I silence within me all the buzzing of domestic worries, of problems with the children, of various jobs to finish. I try to free myself from all that, so as to make myself available to my husband in heart, mind, and soul, ready to listen to his worries, his thoughts, his difficulties. And afterwards we may talk about our children, about my worries, or my work, but we do it in a purified atmosphere.

"Reflection on our married life was my first initiation into mental prayer.

"Several times when I had the feeling of treading in place, I wanted to delve into St. Teresa, for example, but then something would keep me from it. I then understood that there is another biography to consult, the biography every married couple writes together day by day."

* * *

And now that I have shown you the way, Paul and Monique, it is up to you to decipher the parable of your marriage, and to make your own discoveries about it. But following the example of the Apostles, be sure to ask Christ to explain its meaning to you. Otherwise you will be like those of whom the Master said: *"they look but do not see, they listen but do not hear or understand. . . . Sluggish indeed is this people's heart . . . they have firmly closed their eyes; otherwise they might . . . understand with their hearts, and turn back to me, and I should heal them"* (Mt 13:13, 15).

34. To a young man engaged to be married

My dear François, in my last letter I invited you to take advantage of the privileged time of your engagement to discover the riches and demands of love, so that you can build your marriage on a solid foundation. But your union with Christ should also benefit immensely from this wonderful experience of betrothal.

I know, of course, that it is sometimes said that the hearts and minds of an engaged couple are closed to everyone else. That's true in the case of a selfish, possessive, and carnal love. But it is not true of real Christians. Their love, on the contrary, opens their hearts and minds to others, to the world, and to God. I have often seen for myself that this is so.

May your engagement be a path that leads to God! May it inspire you to give him thanks for your happiness and ask for his help! Above all, may it enable you to advance deeper into the knowledge and love of Christ!

Life with Christ (especially during mental prayer) is also a dialogue of love, a spiritual encounter, and a communion of souls. Admittedly, sensibility and emotion play a great role in the love of an egaged couple. The soul's love for Christ, on the other hand, while not excluding nuances of sensibility and affectivity, is rooted above all in faith. The fact remains that the same fundamental laws are at work at all levels of love.

A letter I recently received illustrates what I have just said:

* * *

"My habit of always beginning my mental prayer by offering God my joy, goes back to the distant days of my engagement to be married.

And this is how it came about. When Bernadette and I were together, I would be terribly unhappy if I sensed that she was not happy. I was equally wretched when, in her letter, she failed to say that our separation was hard for her. On the other hand, when we were together, I was filled with intense happiness if she seemed to radiate joy. I was very happy, too, when she wrote me of her sadness at being away from me.

"These reactions began to worry me. Why did I need her to be happy when she was near, and unhappy when we were apart? Were these not mediocre, egocentric feelings, revealing self-love rather than a disinterested love for her? I remember mulling this question over and over until one day I saw the light: to love another person is to want that person to be happy. When contemplating marriage, one must ask oneself whether one is capable of making the other happy, or being the other's happiness. Anyone who did not ask himself the question with a certain anxiety could not be genuinely in love.

"The day I understood this, I was freed from all anxiety and scruples, and I was as proud as if I had been the first to make the discovery. The next day, when Bernadette asked me what she could do to make me happy, I had my answer ready. 'Nothing except to be happy yourself; happy over my presence and my love; happy over me. Your joy that I read so often in your face and in your eyes, the joy I guess at in your heart, that is the most wonderful gift you can offer me.'

"That evening, as I prayed by my bed before retiring, a thought suddenly came to me. If the most Bernadette can do to make me happy is to offer me her joy over being loved by me, then there is probably nothing better I can do to make God happy than offer him my joy in his presence, in his love, and in his happiness. I quickly realized that this joy on my part was not very strong, and I was deeply ashamed. I promised myself to visit with my God more assiduously, so that this joy might grow within me, and so that my offering might become more pleasing to him.

"Many years have gone by. I have rarely missed my daily mental prayer, and I always begin by offering up my joy. Not the least benefit of this, is that I am brought each day to ask myself the question: is God really my joy? If I notice that this joy is decreasing, I know what conclusion to draw. I must become more attentive to my God's love for me."

* * *

My dear François, that is only an example. At least it has the merit of clearly showing how human love, in one of its aspects, can be an invitation to divine love. But there is also the need to live this human love well, to recognize its riches and demands, and to discern the allusions within it to the world of divine grace.

35. The arid garden

Y ou write: "My mental prayer is arid, and it seems that my life is no longer bearing fruit as it did at the start of my priestly ministry. But I cannot understand the reason why." Your letter reached me here in the rural rectory where I am spending a short vacation. I have been reading and rereading it in my darkened room, the shutters closed because of the torrid sun outside. And the vegetable garden under my window is in a sorry state: everything is burned to a crisp. My pastor friend laments that he will have no vegetables this year. A good heavy rain is needed. But day after day passes, and the sky remains implacably blue.

Is this not perhaps what is also lacking in your soul? Rain, the rain that is the word of God? The comparison did not originate with me, but with Isaiah:

* * *

> "For just as from the heavens
>   the rain and the snow come down
> And do not return there
>   till they have watered the earth,
>   making it fertile and fruitful,
> Giving seed to him who sows
>   and bread to him who eats,
> So shall my word be
>   that goes forth from my mouth;
> It shall not return to me void,
>   but shall do my will,
>   achieving the end for which I sent it."

(Is 55:10-11)

* * *

Although the farmer can do nothing to obtain the rain he needs, you have only to will it and the word of God will make your life fruitful. God's word can never fail us. We are the ones who fail God's word.

Your decision to give up your meditation of Scripture over the past few months makes me wonder—and makes me ask you—whether you have the requisite esteem for the word of God.

You tell me that you are no longer able to meditate. If you defined the word "meditate" in its fundamental sense of "reflecting on," reflecting on God's word, delving into its underlying meaning, you could no longer claim that you are unqualified to meditate. Of course, you still have to put it into practice, and with greater perseverance since your active and overburdened life does not lend itself to meditation.

True, you assure me that you strive to create silence within you, to hollow out a void within yourself. And I understand that you do so in order to make room for God. But aren't you making a mistake about this? Silence has no value in its own right. What matters is not to silence the noises within one's soul, but to listen to God's word, the *"word of life"* (Ph 2:16), the *"message of salvation"* (Ac 13:26), to *"listen to the word,"* (Mk 4:20), to *"retain it"* (Lk 8:15), to *"be true"* to it (Jn 8:51; 14:23). It is the word which, penetrating into the soul, will eliminate the noise and create silence.

It is not a matter of first creating an interior void, either. Father Plé writes perceptively:

* * *

"We see the error of many who think that to place oneself in the presence of God consists simply in making a void within one's soul of all earthly concerns. All extraneous thoughts are hastily suppressed, somewhat the way a policeman quickly evacuates a room through which a public figure will soon pass, and whom the policeman precedes and protects. Then, assuming one can empty one's head and heart, one awaits a "feeling" of the presence of God. Nothing happens, except perhaps the illusion of it."

* * *

I am well aware that spiritual writers recommend mental prayer of silence and emptiness, during which one must stop talking, reasoning, and acting. St. John of the Cross describes this mental prayer in a very compelling way: "Attention simply and solely fixed on one's object—the way someone opens his eyes to look out with love." But this passive, contemplative mental prayer is a gift from God. One cannot attain to it by one's own efforts. If it is not given to us, we have better things to do than to groan, await it idly, and watch for its coming or its return.

There is no wind? Then grasp the oars if you want to get out into the open sea. God is not talking to you in the depths of your heart? Listen to him in the Scriptures. Seek his word, chew it, masticate it; in a word, meditate.

So you see, prayer is God's word, not in its movement from God to man, but in its return from man to God. It is the word of God coming back to God, having achieved its mission, *"the end for which it was sent out,"* as Isaiah tells us.

When you are nourished with the word of God, everything within you, like a garden after the rain, will turn green again and grow. Life, the life of God, the theological life, will spring up again. *Faith* will dwell in your soul: faith—that alert, eager knowledge, filled with wonder, of the mystery of God and his love, a knowledge that is always young because it is renewed every day. And because love calls out to love, *charity* will spring up in its turn, the more fervent in proportion to the vitality of your faith. And the *hope* of knowing and loving God more and more, of seeing his Kingdom come upon earth, will be the stimulus to your mental prayer, and indeed to everything you do.

36. *"Listen to him"* (Mt 17:5)

Although the Gospels offer us countless sayings of Christ, they record for us only three statements of the Father. We should hold them very precious! One of them is a counsel, the one and only counsel of the Father to his children. Should we not receive it with infinite, intensely filial deference, and obey it with the greatest zeal? This counsel, which contains the secret of all holiness, is expressed in three simple words: *"Listen to him"* (Mt 17:5). That is what the Father says in pointing out his beloved Son to us.

To engage in mental prayer is thus the great act of obedience to the Father. It is to sit like Mary of Bethany at the feet of Christ to listen to his words, or better still, to listen to him speaking to us. Indeed, we must be attentive to him, even more than to his words.

It follows that it is very commendable to engage in mental prayer based on a page of Scripture. We must not read this page like a professor of literature, but like a woman in love who listens to the heartbeat of her lover beyond the words written in the letters she receives from him.

It is a great art to know how to listen. Christ has told us so himself: *"Take heed, therefore, how you hear"* (Lk 8:18). If we are like a footpath, or rocky ground, or soil choked with briers and thorns (cf. Lk 8:5-8), his word cannot grow within us. We need to be like good soil where the seed that is sown finds all that it needs to sprout, develop and ripen.

Besides, listening is not solely the work of the intellect. Our whole being, soul and body, mind and heart, imagination, memory, and will, must be attentive to Christ's words. We must welcome them and make room for them. Our whole being must allow itself to be surrounded, penetrated, and possessed by Christ's words, and accept them totally, without reservation.

You understand why I use the word "listen" in preference to "meditate." It has a more evangelistic tone, and above all it describes not a solitary activity but an encounter, an exchange, a heart-to-heart talk. And this is essentially what mental prayer is.

The truth is, that without grace nobody would be able to listen to Christ, because we are all born deaf, children of a race afflicted with deafness. But at the time of our baptism, Christ pronounced the word which—since the healing of the deaf-mute of the Decapolis—has opened the ears of millions of disciples: *"Ephphatha!"* (*"Be opened!"*) (Mk 7:34).

When we grant Christ's word access through mental prayer, it converts us, makes us *"pass from life to death"* (cf. Jn 5:24), and brings us back to life. It becomes in us, for us, a gushing spring of eternal life.

But it is not enough to listen to the word. Christ tells us that *"blest are they who hear the word of God and keep it"* (Lk 11:28). Blest are they who delight in it and are nourished by it, who carry it about with them the way Mary carried the child she had conceived—he who is the subsistent Word. Through his Mother, Jesus sanctified those whom she encountered, causing John the Baptist to leap for joy in Elizabeth's womb. He wants to do the same through us.

And that is still not saying enough. Once heard and kept, this word *"must be carried out in practice"* (cf. Jm 1:25). Understand this to mean that we must be attentive to Christ's dynamic presence within us throughout the day. We must be eager to follow his suggestions and inspirations. It is the dynamism of the word that will make us multiply good works, and which will inspire us to toil, suffer, and die for the coming of the Father's Kingdom. If we are faithful, our joy will be great because Jesus has said, *"My mother and my brothers are those who hear the word of God and act upon it"* (Lk 8:21).

37. *"The unfathomable riches of Christ"* (Ep 3:8)

I am happy to learn of your resolve to make a retreat. Nothing is more important for you at this moment than to introduce mental prayer into your life. In so doing, you are entering on a magnificent and awesome adventure, about which only love can give you some idea. In the course of this adventure, you will encounter the greatest joys and the harshest trials. "Joys and trials": these words are too weak. You will discover the very meaning of your life, and if you play the game without cheating—which involves giving Christ total power over you—you will know the unique plenitude that only the greatest love can bring.

To come back to your letter and your request, "Would you be willing to guide me?" While I do not hesitate to say "Yes," I did ruminate at some length over the advice to give you. Should I begin by telling you about the different forms and methods of mental prayer? Should I speak to you of the prime movers of prayer: praise, adoration, repentance, and petition? My own reflection (and even more, the experience of those I have watched set out with a sure compass on the path of mental prayer) has provided me with the subject matter for this first letter.

Do you want to learn how to pray? Then seek to know Christ. I am not speaking of a purely intellectual knowledge, but of a knowledge in faith and love. And first of all, you must believe firmly that Christ is not a figure lost in the mists of history. He is a living person, *The Living Person*, who stands at your door and knocks, as he himself has said.

This is the Christ you must seek to understand—the Christ who is reaching out to you to form a personal relationship with you. You must strive to know what he thinks and wants of you, and what his sentiments are toward you. There is only one way to keep you from going astray in speculation or in illusions. It is to grab hold of your Gospel and never let it go, and then seek untiringly. Little by little, the true face of Christ will reveal itself to you with increasing clarity, and with the help of his grace (for he is in even a greater hurry to make himself known than you are to know him) you will discover *"the unfathomable riches"* of his love, about which St. Paul speaks (cf. Ep 3:8).

When mental prayer is understood in this way, the problem is already solved (indeed, it is often badly stated) as to whether mental prayer should be meditation. If meditation is defined as a rigorous method, then it is not a requisite, although it may be useful to certain temperaments. If meditation is conceived as an intellectual exercise unrelated to love, then it must be avoided as a truncated and dangerous form of mental prayer. "Woe to the knowledge that is not impelled to love." But if meditation is understood to be the eager search for the knowledge of Christ, that love demands and constantly inspires (because the one who loves untiringly seeks to know more in order to love more), then "Yes!", a thousand times "Yes!", mental prayer must be meditation.

I am sure that many Christians are discouraged from persevering in mental prayer because they do not succeed in loving Christ. If they don't love him, it is because they are not trying to know him. One does not love a shadow, or somebody one does not know. Only the discovery of Christ's astounding love for us can make love and prayer well up in our hearts.

In counseling you to begin by seeking to know Christ, I have the sense of toeing the line of divine pedagogy. Isn't that the way God went about drawing the apostles and disciples to himself? Jesus came to them, offering them his wonderful friendship. They saw him, touched him and heard him. They were conquered and gave themselves to him. Then, one day, Christ left them after saying these disconcerting words: *"It is much better for you that I go"* (Jn 16:7).

It is true, nonetheless, that Christ's friendship was the decisive experience of their lives. The same applies to the life of mental prayer. It is meant to lead Christians to a very lofty union with God. But it can have no better starting point, or firmer support, than the knowledge of the unbelievable love, both human and divine, that Christ is offering us.

38. The deepest book

I think you are wrong to read during your mental prayer. Rather than nourishing your prayer life, it flatters your taste—not to say your gluttony—for ideas. Why don't you put all books aside? Or better, you should be content with "the deepest book," as the Curé of Ars called it one day when he was singing its praises.

This is what he said:

* * *

"The cross is the deepest book anyone can ever read. Those who do not know it are ignorant, even if they should happen to know all other books. The only real scholars are those who love it, consult it, and deepen their understanding of it. Bitter as this book may be, we are never happier than when we drown in its bitterness. The more we follow its teaching, the more we want to continue following it. When reading it, time flies. We learn all we want to know, and we never have enough of what we discover in it."

* * *

I can guess your answer. "The language of this book is foreign to me." It's up to you to learn it. A Christian has no right to be ignorant of it. It is the language of God. Look at all the men and women of prayer, all the saints pictured for us in Christian iconography (engravings, colored prints, illuminated manuscripts, and paintings). They are shown at the foot of the Cross, or with a crucifix in their hands, engrossed in deciphering its message. Is it not obvious that from now on no book can possibly deter them from meditating on the Cross, "the Beloved's love letter to us"?

39. Should we pray before the crucifix?

Madam, rest assured, your letter did not scandalize me at all. You are not wrong to ask yourself whether it is wise to have your young children pray before the image of the crucified Christ, whether there is a danger that the image of the Crucified may perturb their emotions.

You are right, however, in holding suspect the motives that lead many Christians of our own day to become alienated from the crucifix, to neglect the Lord's Passion in favor of his Resurrection. As if the Resurrection did not require passage through death! They are far removed from the mind of St. Paul, who declared to the Corinthians, *"I determined that while I was with you I would speak of nothing but Jesus Christ and him crucified"* (1 Cor 2:2).

The Christian conscience has been asking the same question as you, with varying degrees of acuity, throughout the twenty centuries of our era. Christian art bears witness to it, and especially the history of the iconography of the crucified Christ: paintings, sculptures, calvaries, crucifixes, etc.

During the first six centuries of the Christian era, Christ was rarely depicted on the Cross. The image of the Good Shepherd was for the Christians of that time what the Crucified is for us today. Subsequently, the Crucifixion became a privileged theme of Christian iconography. There were more and more crucifixes. We see them in the statuary of the cathedrals. They were enshrined in all Christian homes, and in hospitals and schools. They rose up at crossroads and in public squares. Alas! Their production often became a commercial venture, and the Christian people were submerged by these crucifixes devoid of artistic and spiritual quality. Even the representations of the Crucified by genuine artists were sometimes ambivalent, at times more sensual than spiritual. I am thinking now of certain Renaissance painters.

Even truly Christian artists have had divergent conceptions. These can be reduced to two, allowing for some simplification: the "realistic" and the "mystical." Depending on the time and place, they have been received with varying degrees of enthusiasm.

The realistic formula is not the first in point of time. It was slow in gaining acceptance. It seeks above all to express the physical and moral sufferings of Christ. The artists portray him unclothed. His body is lacerated, tortured, distorted with pain to the point of being an unspeakably pitiful remnant of humanity. On his head rests a tragic crown of thorns. These artists seek first of all to arouse the emotions, to awaken compassion, and perhaps to inspire horror for sin. They also intend to encourage Christians to unite their own sufferings to those of Christ. Some of these crucifixes seem empty of all religious content. One has the impression of looking at the symbol of mankind's distress, rather than at the sign of man's salvation through the incarnate Son of God.

The creators of these crucifixes speak of human and historical truth. In fact, "realistic" crucifixes tend to adulterate the truth, or at least to neglect one of its essential aspects. They represent the man who suffers but not the God who triumphs, the tortures of the flesh but not the victory of love. If Christ had offered only the spectacle of human suffering, if he had been simply a pitiful remnant of humanity, would the centurion standing right in front of him have cried out, *"Clearly this man was the Son of God!"* (Mk 15:39)?

The so-called "mystical" crucifixes express a contrary conception. They portray Christ clothed, sometimes even with a long tunic, and with a crown on his head, usually a crown of thorns, but sometimes an imperial crown. His eyes are wide open, expressing strength of soul and serenity. His face has a halo of glory, and sometimes it is imbued with an infinite pity for men. His arms are horizontal, his body is straight. The artists want to remind us that the Crucified is first of all God, the living God, conqueror of suffering and death, and that his sacrifice is voluntary.

Such artistic works tend less to arouse our emotions than to stimulate our faith in the divinity of Christ, and in his victory. They seek to awaken our hope rather than our compassion, to convince us that the Passion was but a passage toward the Resurrection. Some of these crucifixes are cold and emotionless, but there are others from which emanate great tenderness, gentleness, and radiant peace. It is their immense merit not to veil the essential, to allow us to have an intuition of the divine mystery.

Do these few notes on the history of art provide you with a preliminary answer to the questions you are asking me?

To eliminate the crucifix from our churches and our homes would be a frightful religious regression. So be sure to teach your children to pray before the crucifix. For, as the Curé of Ars used to say, it is "the deepest book." But it is no less true that you must choose among the crucifixes or images of Christ crucified. Ruthlessly reject those that might perturb the emotions of young children, or betray the underlying truth of the sacrifice of Jesus Christ. In addition, since your children will often be seeing vulgar crucifixes, or crucifixes expressing a non-religious realism, teach them to look at them all with the eyes of a faith that discerns the mystery beyond any imperfect or misleading artistic expression.

Under such conditions, the crucifix will deliver its true message to your children. It will no longer appear as the apotheosis of suffering, but indeed as the sign of the greatest love. This is the love of the Father, who loved men to the point of *giving* them his Son. This is the Son's love for his Father, and the Savior's love for men, his brothers. *"There is no greater love than this: to lay down one's life for one's friends"* (Jn 15:13).

It will appear as the apotheosis of joy, too—yes, of the most overpowering joy, for Christ has said, *"There is greater joy in giving than in receiving"* (Ac 20:35).

"Christ is living in me"
(Gal 2:20)

Christian prayer is not a merely human activity. It is a mysterious divine reality. It is the very prayer of the Son of God implanted into man's heart.

Whether we know it or not, we are present to the prayer of Christ. To engage in mental prayer is to take our place in the heart of the praying Christ.

40 *"I have prayed for you"* (Lk 22:32)—In moments of discouragement, cowardice, or vertigo, when the wellsprings of our prayer have dried up, prayer is still possible. This is the prayer that we ask Christ to address to the Father for us, in our name.

41 *He intercedes for us unceasingly* (cf. Heb 7:25)—But Christ wants more than that. Not content to pray for us, he wants to unite us to himself in love, so that we may live by his life and pray with his own prayer.

42 *"If only you recognized God's gift!"* (Jn 4:10)—Thus, prayer consists in surrendering ourselves totally to the sanctifying energies of the glorious Christ who is constantly making, out of all creatures, one vast body vibrating with his filial prayer.

43 *"And Christ will give you light"* (Ep 5:14)—In fact, in the prayer of each Christian, poor as it may appear, the Father discerns the very prayer of his beloved Son.

44 *It is no longer I who pray . . .*—This prayer of Christ within us is seed sown among thorns. It is our job to foster its growth by pruning the vegetation of our thoughts and our teeming desires, that are constantly threatening to choke it.

45 *Seed sown among thorns*—Little by little, and in the measure that

we cleave to it with our whole mind and heart, Christ's prayer becomes more intense and takes possession of our whole being.

46   *It is Christ who prays in me*—To practice mental prayer does not consist so much in producing a prayer, as in making contact within us with a full-fledged prayer, the living prayer of Christ.

47   *His prayer is my prayer*—His prayer is right there, quivering with the filial tenderness of the Son for his Father, to whom it invites us to speak in words bold beyond imagining: "Abba, beloved Father!"

48   *Beloved Father*—It is the Holy Spirit's task to identify us with Christ, so that we may say in complete truth, "I live, I pray, but it is no longer I, it is Christ who lives and prays within me."

49   *Veni—Come*

40. *"I have prayed for you"* (Lk 22:32)

I am apprehensive about writing to you. In the face of certain griefs, there is little one can do but pray and be silent. The slightest advice runs the risk of doing more harm than good. It is so easy to give advice.

I shall therefore limit myself to relating to you what an aged missionary once told me, after he had spent more than forty years in the bush.

He was then taking a needed rest on his brother's farm in the mountains of France's Haut-Jura. As we sauntered through this austere and beautiful region of pastures and pine woods, he would tell me with amazing verve of his memories of the bush country, memories more exciting than an adventure novel. One day, he suddenly turned serious as he recalled a particular episode of his life. He might never have divulged it to me, if I had not questioned him about the role of mental prayer in the life of a missionary.

He began to speak.

* * *

"I had been at the Mission about six years, when suddenly the rising tide of temptation took hold of me like a boat abandoned on the beach. Irresistibly, it grabbed me, lifted me up, threw me back, and grabbed me again. I tried to pray but couldn't. The desperate child was trying to reach his Father, and was powerless to do so.

"I don't know how or why, but after several days of exhausting struggle, a prayer literally came out of me, as suddenly as a partridge flies out of the bushes. I cried out to Jesus Christ: 'You see I can't pray any more! Well then, it's up to you. Pray for me, come now, pray for me!'

"Almost at once, calm returned to me. I couldn't believe it. At first, I thought it was a calm before a more terrible attack. Then, I soon became convinced that I have been heard, and that Christ was saying to me, as he had to Peter, *'I have prayed for you that your faith may never fail. You in turn must strengthen your brothers'* (Lk 22:32). Certainly, I have experienced other hours of temptation since then, but never again the anguished feeling of being the plaything of a violent and all-powerful tempest.

"It is hard to find words to translate the intensity of this experience. I can't express the spontaneity, the vehemence, and the imperiousness of my cry to Christ: 'Come now, pray for me!'

"If you only knew what it is like, after having learned in books that Christ prays for all men, to discover all of a sudden, in the midst of a desperate situation, that he is there. Someone real is by my side, and in place of my faltering prayer, he, the beloved Son, prays for me, interceding personally before the Father for me!

"*'I have prayed for you.'* In the most desperate moments, it sufficed to recall these words, for peace to reign within my soul."

41. *"He intercedes for us unceasingly"* (cf. Heb 7:25)

There is no need for you to worry when, after your mental prayer is concluded, you remember that you have not prayed explicitly for your husband or your children. To be busy with God is never to neglect one's loved ones. What we give to God is never taken away from others.

I don't mean to say that it is useless to pray for those we love. It is an imperative duty. Christ's own example leaves no doubt about that. But I ask you not to have scruples when your hour of mental prayer has been spent as if only God and you existed. Besides, isn't this the best way of praying for your loved one? Forget everything, including them, to devote yourself more completely to your search for God, and enter more deeply into his friendship.

Do you think God cannot find, present in your heart of a wife and mother, those whom you fear you are forsaking for him? When you are closer to God, then they, too, are nearer to him. Through your prayer, the little "mystical body" that is your family seeks God and sings his praises.

Through your prayer, your entire family drinks from the Wellspring.

If you really understand what I am saying to you, you are very close to entering into the loftier mystery of Christ's own prayer. Just as the Father can find within your soul all those whom you love, so, too, he sees in the vast heart of his Son at prayer all the men and women for whom the Son gave his life. And that is why Christ's prayer is so important for us. Through his prayer, we come close to the Father and praise him. In his prayer, we drink deep of the Holy Spirit, who, the Gospel of John teaches us, springs forth like a torrent of living water from the love between the Father and the Son.

If it is true that a mother's prayer is already the great treasure of her children, how much more is the prayer of Jesus Christ our incomparable riches! How secure we would be, if we really believed that the glorious Christ at the right hand of the Father intercedes for us unceasingly, as the Epistle to the Hebrews affirms (Heb 7:25)!

To go to mental prayer is to join in Christ's own prayer. It is to find our place once more within the heart of Christ praying to his Father.

42. "If only you recognized God's gift!" (Jn 4:10)

Never forget that in order to go to God, we must pass through Christ. Don't let this word "pass" mislead you. It is not a question of going beyond Christ to reach God, as if God were waiting for us on the other side of Christ. It is only through Christ, with Christ, and *in* Christ that we can find the Father. That is why there is never anything better to do than to love Christ. That is why you have no need to fear that your mental prayer (which—you tell me—is a dialogue with Christ) will keep you away from the Father. *"Philip, you still do not know that whoever has seen me has seen the Father?"* (cf. Jn 14:9).

So let the friendship of Christ envelop you, take hold of you, and permeate you. But understand well this friendship that has arisen in your life in such an unexpected way.

You will find in it all the riches of human friendship, for Christ is truly man. His human nature is not merely a disguise temporarily assumed, and then thrown away after thirty-three years on this earth. The Son of God really became *flesh*, and he loves us with a heart of flesh, not with a love from some other world that we cannot understand.

Or rather, he does love us with a divine love that is altogether different from human love. But this love, to make itself understood, borrowed a man's heart and expressed itself in human language. This word "human" is to be understood in a very encompassing sense. Not only did the Son of God *tell* us of his love with words (*"I no longer speak of you as slaves, . . . Instead, I call you friends"* (Jn 15:15). He went further, and *manifested* his love by his attitudes and actions. Think about this:

Some women came to Jesus, holding their children out to him so he could bless them. The Apostles, being serious men with no time for foolishness, reprimanded them. Then Jesus grasped these unkempt children, and took them into his arms as a sign of protest. It was as if to say, "Why would you refuse me this pleasure of dialoguing with these tiny children through looks and words?" (cf. Mk 10:13-16).

And when Luke shows us Christ as he encountered the pitiable procession carrying the only son of a widow to the cemetery, and tells us that Jesus was *"moved with pity,"* how can we doubt that Christ felt sorrow when he saw this tearful mother? (Cf. Lk 7:11-17).

Even more revealing is the scene recorded by St. John. When Jesus saw Mary overcome with sorrow over her brother's death, *"he was troubled in spirit, moved by the deepest emotions"* and *"began to weep."* The Jews were not mistaken when they commented, *"See how much he loved him!"* (Jn 11:33-36).

The profound humanity of Christ's heart is made known to us in so many passages of the Gospels! His heart is so much more human than ours. We have so much trouble finding a middle ground between an overly human sensibility that is quickly out of control, and an inhuman self-control that becomes inflexible in order not to give in to emotion.

When you come close to Christ in mental prayer, let your faith strive to recognize his friendship. Let it be filled with wonder as it enumerates the unsearchable resources of his tenderness. Because Jesus loves you, he desires your presence and cannot fail to rejoice at your coming to him. Because he loves you, he is impatient to shower his benefactions on you. As he himself has said from his own experience, *"There is more happiness in giving than receiving"* (Ac 20:35). And more happiness in forgiving than in giving. Because he loves you, he sympathizes in the strongest sense of the word: he *communes* with all of your sentiments.

Dare to believe that, in Christ's love for us, all the nuances of human love are to be found. Believe that it is vibrant, cordial, warm, eager, and compassionate. You will be giving homage to the truth of the Incarnation. The hunted priest in Graham Greene's *The Power and the Glory* did not discern this:

"It would be enough to scare us—God's love. It set fire to a bush in the desert, didn't it, and smashed open graves and set the dead walking in the dark? Oh, a man like me would run a mile to get away if he felt that love around."

That is admirably put, and it is true in a certain sense. But what the priest fails to see is that this love (precisely in order to approach us without shocking us, in order to familiarize us with it—I feel like saying, "in order to tame us") has revealed its Splendor to us, but filtered through the face of a man. It communicates its riches to us, but through the heart of a man.

Do not raise the objection that Christ is risen. While the Resurrection delivered him from the servitudes of mortal flesh—from fatigue and thirst, from sadness and anguish—it did not strip him of his tender and magnanimous humanity. Glory does not destroy nature, but perfects it.

That is why we must go to Christ with the trust of those Jewish children who refused to be deterred by the Apostles' taunts.

On the other hand, we must avoid seeking only a wonderfully human friendship in our relationship with Christ. He offers us more. And so we, too, must hope for more when we come to him.

"When friendship does not encounter equality, it creates it." Christ has verified this ancient adage. The love of the Son of God moves him to give us a share in his incomparable dignity. He wants to make us, children of the earth that we are, children of God. But to accomplish this, we must be reborn by Water and the Spirit. We must open ourselves, through the sacraments and prayer, to Christ's divinizing action. We must be reborn, and not just once, but every day and at every moment. That is why it is a deadly mistake to separate ourselves from Christ. That is why we must maintain our contact with him, which only love can establish and preserve. Mental prayer is a privileged moment in this contact with Christ.

Why do Christians find it so hard to establish the link between two fundamental attitudes toward Christ? One sees him as the brother, the friend with the understanding and generous heart, and the other sees the eternal Son of God as the source of all holiness. Christ is both man and God. There can be no question of separating and choosing. We cannot turn first to his human friendship, and then to his divinizing action. We cannot alternate between one and the other.

Since grace invites you to seek Christ's friendship, do not hesitate. Come close to him. Offer yourself to the love of his heart, meek and humble, tender and strong. And do not look elsewhere to find the loftiest gifts of God. It is through the human tenderness of Christ that the torrent of divine life will pour into you. That is the great invention of God's love. It is through a fleshly, human heart, the heart of Christ, that this love has decided to transmit to us the life that wells up eternally within the communion of the Triune God.

43. *"And Christ will give you light"* (Ep 5:14)

Your letter is on my desk. I was uncertain how to answer it. A visit from a friend has saved the day. As it happens, it seems that his experience can throw light on your own.

I had not seen him for a year, as he lives in southern France and rarely comes to Paris. During his last visit he confided to me that he practiced mental prayer, but with difficulty. He has remained faithful to it. He devotes a half hour to it each day, in spite of his very busy life as a doctor and father of a family. He said to me, "It is my strength and my balance wheel." I responded, "And yet I remember that last year it was an austere effort devoid of benefit, according to your own words. What caused the change?" "St. Paul. I have been constantly reading the Epistles of the Captivity: Ephesians and Colossians."

I was intrigued, and got him to talk about it at length. I shall try to convey to you his eager accent of conviction, to show you how the thought of the great Apostle (having attained admirable maturity in the evening of his life in a Roman prison) can illumine and guide your mental prayer.

Once again it was the threat of heresy that goaded Paul's thinking, and made it leap to new heights. At Colossae, some of the faithful were tempted to rash speculations inspired by the Hellenistic philosophies that attributed to certain heavenly beings, intermediate between God and men, great powers over the progress of the world. These theories threatened to put Christ's role in eclipse. Now, to question the absolute supremacy of Christ was to attack St. Paul at his most sensitive point. Immediately, his thought quivered, and was galvanized into action. He delved into the mystery of the mission of his Lord as he had never done before, and he constructed a vigorous synthesis. His contemplation now reached heights never before attained, and he paused in awe before new, vastly expanded horizons.

At the heart of Paul's synthesis: the humanity of Christ, triumphant and glorified, in whom *"the fullness of deity resides"* (Col 2:9). This humanity shines out over our universe. It is our world's spiritual sun, and no human being escapes its irradiation.

The entire sanctifying power of God is concentrated, but not imprisoned, in this risen Christ. Concentrated in order to be infinitely diffused, in order to take hold of all the men and women who offer themselves to its action, and make of them new, divinized beings. Diffused in order to form out of them a vast Body quivering with the Spirit of the Son, and with the prayer that this Spirit breathes into it: "Father, Father!"

I say, "all men and women," but it is truly the whole universe that St. Paul sees as subject to Christ's influence, and placed under his dominion. This divine power, concentrated in the glorious humanity of Christ, wills to extend to the farthest limits of the cosmos, to take possession of everything and gather it up toward the Father.

These are the perspectives that transformed my friend's mental prayer. When the vast Pauline synthesis passes before our eyes (that is, when we know that we are in the presence of the glorious Christ everywhere and always), prayer consists essentially in surrendering ourselves, with open minds and hearts, to his unceasing action and control.

Through the process of photosynthesis, a tree nourishes itself with light. The soul, through mental prayer, draws its nourishment from Christ, as well as its cohesion and unity "to achieve its growth in God." And little by little, all the areas of its interior universe are penetrated and conquered by the vital influx of the One who wants to be *"all in all"* (cf. Ep. 4:6).

I do hope these views may be of great help to you, too. I leave you with this verse from the Epistle to the Ephesians, which is generally thought to be a fragment of a hymn sung in the early Church:

> *"Awake, O sleeper,*
> *arise from the dead,*
> *and Christ will give you light."*

(Ep 5:14)

44. It is no longer I who pray . . .

I can well understand the feeling that impelled you to write to me: "My daily mental prayer seems laughable to me. I cannot imagine that this stammering prayer of a miniscule creature could interest the perfect and infinite God." You are keenly aware of the wretchedness of creatures, and of the majesty of God. That is a precious and essential insight of faith. It is certainly a gift of grace. But there is another insight of faith that I would like you to grasp, so as to give you a lofty opinion of your daily mental prayer, miserable as it may seem to you.

Let's begin by getting a broader perspective. Before speaking of your personal mental prayer, let us talk about Christ's mental prayer. Bérulle, in a passage that I particularly like, celebrates the uniqueness of the prayer of Jesus Christ:

* * *

"From all eternity, there was indeed an infinitely adorable God, but there was not yet an infinite adorer. There was certainly a God worthy of being infinitely loved and served, but there was no infinite man or servant capable of rendering an infinite service and giving an infinite love. O Jesus, you are now that adorer, that man, that servant, infinite in power, in quality, and in dignity, fully adequate for this duty and for this divine homage. You are this man who loves, adores, and serves the supreme majesty as it deserves to be loved, served, and honored."

* * *

This text reminds us of Jesus withdrawing to the solitude of the mountains during the night, in order to pray. And above all, it reminds us of Calvary, where the perfect adorer offered God perfect worship.

Should we ask ourselves whether the perfect prayer of Jesus rendered the prayer of ordinary men and women futile, and definitively superseded it?

We can quickly answer that this prayer of Christ, far from obviating the prayers of the human race (all those stammering prayers since the origins of mankind, all the sacrifices of all religions and all eras), gathers them into itself and offers them to God. In Christ's prayer, and through it, they have admirable meaning and efficacy.

But there is a still more wonderful answer. Christ wants his prayer to resound throughout the universe. He wants the most ordinary Christian at prayer to have much more to offer than hesitant words and awkward sentiments. He wants him to have access to the very prayer of the Son of God. He wants all men and women to be able to take possession of his prayer, make it their own, and present it to God.

But that is still not saying enough. Jesus Christ does not merely want his prayer to be our own as a possession which we are free to dispose of. He wants his prayer to be implanted into the innermost depths of our being, to be the soul of our soul, so that we can in all truth repeat after St. Paul: *"The life I live now is not my own . . ."* (Gal 2:20). I pray, but it is no longer I who pray, but Christ who prays within me. It is the Spirit of the Son, the Holy Spirit, who makes the filial cry, *"Abba, Father!"*, resound in me. And so Christ's prayer, far from supplanting the prayer of men and women, wonderfully increases its value.

During the Easter Vigil, in the darkened church, the flame of the paschal candle is communicated little by little to the multitude of little candles held in the hands of the faithful. In the same way, Christ, through baptism, gradually wins men and women to himself all over the world, and makes his filial prayer rise up in and from their souls.

It is his Son that the Father recognizes in all the baptized. Laughable as their prayer may seem to be, the Father recognizes in it the prayer of his own Son.

45. Seed sown among thorns

I wholeheartedly encourage your desire to learn to pray and to seek counsel in the works of the great spiritual writers. But I think I discern a certain fever, a certain excess in your eagerness. You seem to be acting as if prayer were one of man's conquests, when it is above all a grace received from Christ.

He came into our midst in order to teach us to pray. He didn't come merely to give us a formula for prayer, even the supreme formula, the Lord's Prayer. He came to teach us his own prayer which, before being articulated, is first of all the heart of his being: praise, filial love and intercession. How can I say "teach"? He came to communicate his prayer to us, and infuse it into us. He never ceases accomplishing an invisible mission among us. This consists in implanting into our hearts his prayer, the only prayer that can really gain a hearing before the Father.

Every soul in the state of grace has *the potentiality for prayer*. It suffices for this potency to pass into *the act of prayer*, for the prayer of Christ, within it and through it, to rise up toward the Father.

But the prayer of Christ, that baptism communicates to us, is a seed sown within us. It is like the mustard seed of the parable, that can become the largest of shrubs, although it is the smallest seed of all. Do not object that this parable is not concerned with the prayer of Christ within the soul, but refers to the Kingdom of God in the world. You know very well that the Kingdom of God is Christ's presence. It is Christ's dominion over that portion of mankind which gives itself to him, and thus is also his dominion over your soul. Now, anyone who speaks of the presence of Christ is speaking of the prayer of Christ, because for Christ, to live is to pray.

If Christ's prayer is within us, a seed sown amidst thorns, our initiation into prayer will consist essentially in becoming aware of this prayer and encouraging its development.

At the same time, let us be modest. It is not the earth that produces the seed, nor is it the gardener's activity that produces flowers and fruits. At the very most, the earth and the gardener provide the conditions and the elements required for the germination and growth of the plant. The Christian does not produce the only prayer that is pleasing to the Father, that is, the prayer of the Son. This prayer is a gift of God. And yet, it withers if we do not bring to it the eagerness and cooperation of our whole being. Likewise, it withers if we do not have recourse to the sacraments that nourish it.

Christ's prayer is choked by brambles if, during mental prayer, we do not prune away the thoughts, feelings, and teeming desires that weigh us down.

But if we do what we are supposed to, then we do not need to try so hard, or be so worried. *"This is how it is with the reign of God. A man scatters seed on the ground. He goes to bed and gets up day after day. Through it all the seed sprouts and grows without his knowing how it happens"* (Mk 4:26-27). Let us have confidence. Let us have faith in the prayer of Christ within us, the faith of the farmer who believes in the seed he has sown. Let us also have the patience of the farmer who knows how to wait until summer to harvest his crop.

46. It is Christ who prays within me

At the very beginning of your mental prayer, make an act of faith in the mysterious presence of Christ within you, which is affirmed in Scripture: *"On that day you will know that I am in my Father, and you in me, and I in you"* (Jn 14:20); *"May Christ dwell in your hearts through faith"* (Ep 3:17).

If Christ is living within you, he is praying within you. For Christ, to live is to pray. Join him, take hold of him, and make his prayer your very own. Or rather (for the terms I have just used place too much emphasis on your own activity), let this prayer take hold of you, permeate you, raise you up, and carry you toward the Father. I do not promise that you will be aware of all this. I ask you only to believe in it and, during mental prayer, to renew your union with Christ's prayer. Make room for Christ's prayer, so it can take possession of every fiber of your being, the way fire penetrates wood and makes it incandescent.

To pray is to grant the request that Christ makes of us: "Lend me your intellect, your heart, your whole being—everything that, in a human person, has the capacity to become prayer—so that I may call forth within you the great praise of the Father. Did I come for any other reason than to kindle fire upon the earth, that it might transform all the trees in the forest into flaming torches? This fire is my prayer. Consent to the fire."

Christ is present within the tiny baptized child, just as he is in the great mystic. But the life of Christ in each of them is not at the same stage of development. While the prayer of Christ already vibrates within the soul of the newly-baptized, it is still only rudimentary, a fire barely kindled. It is during the whole course of our life, in the very measure of our cooperation, that Christ's prayer intensifies and gradually takes possession of our whole being.

Our cooperation consists first of all in cleaving with all our will to Christ's prayer within us. But note the very strong sense I give to the word "cleave." It does not indicate a halfhearted consent, a superficial acquiescence. It signifies a total gift of self, the way a log surrenders to the flames to become fire in its turn. Our cooperation also consists in seeking with our whole mind to know the components of Christ's prayer within us (praise, thanksgiving, oblation and intercession), so that we can espouse them more perfectly. You ask me for subjects for meditation. I don't know of any better than these.

The man of prayer does not at first perceive this prayer of Christ within him. He does not see that his faith guarantees it, and that his meditation makes him understand more deeply. This can go on for a long time. Then a day comes—and it is not necessarily during mental prayer—when he discovers Christ's prayer within his soul. Then he is silent. He fears to frighten it off, just as one fears to scare away a bird perched on the windowsill.

Then suddenly he realizes that Christ's prayer has disappeared. He doesn't know quite how it happened—perhaps during a second's inattention on his part. He is sad. It had been wonderful to discover this prayer in the depths of his being. He hopes that he will find it again, perhaps the very next morning when he awakes or during the day when he takes a break from his work.

He should not grieve over it. Christ's prayer is always there, even when we do not perceive it within us. We must return to it through faith. Above all, we must not make an effort during mental prayer to experience it again. To go to prayer for the sake of God's gifts, and not for God himself, is to fail to honor God as is his due. In accordance with his promise (Jn 20:29), the Lord would manifest himself much oftener to us if we were hungry for God himself, and not greedy for his gifts. Most probably, the grace of perceiving Christ's prayer will be given to us again. Perhaps when we know this prayer better, it will no longer slip away from us. Until then, we must not try to seize this prayer, as we would a fleeing bird.

When at last the soul is perfectly stripped of self, it will experience what St. Ignatius of Antioch described in unforgettable terms in his

Letter to the Romans. This letter was written toward the end of his long apostolic life, on a ship taking him to martyrdom. "My passions have been crucified, and I no longer have any appetite for the things of earth. But I hear within me as from a spring of living water the murmur: *Come to the Father.*"

47. His prayer is my prayer

I t makes me very sad to be in the presence of people who would like to pray, and have a secret nostalgia for prayer, but have lost hope and given it up. Some of them carry this nostalgia around inside of them throughout their lives. They remind me of boys who have lost their sense of direction, and can't find their way back to their father's house.

I remember an old priest who told me, "I have never known how to pray." I think of so many men and women who have said to me: "I don't know how to practice mental prayer," "What's the use of continuing, since I can't even get started?" and "Have I ever really prayed?"

Are you going to join the ranks of these people who have become discouraged with mental prayer?

Understand that it is not so much a question of "practicing" mental prayer, as of "making contact" within yourself with a prayer that is already there, full-fledged and in progress. Christian prayer is not so much the work of man, as the work of God within man. Since the day of your baptism, and providing you are in the state of grace, prayer inhabits you. Not, of course, at the level of consciousness, or at the level of feelings or ideas, but deep-down in the innermost reaches of your being, in the interior chamber where the Holy Spirit dwells. Don't you know that you are a *"temple of the Holy Spirit"* (cf. 1 Cor 6:19), and that this Spirit comes to succor you in your weakness? St. Paul assures us that he intercedes for you, and within you, with ineffable groans, and that his intercession coincides with God's desires (cf. Rm 8:26-27).

The Holy Spirit is the Spirit of Christ. That is why his prayer within you is essentially a filial call, a cry of tender affection. St. Paul affirms, *"God has sent forth into our hearts the Spirit of his Son who cries out 'Abba!' "* (Gal 4:6). Now "Abba!" was the colloquial cry of joy and love uttered by little children as they threw their arms around their father: "*Abba,* dearest Daddy!"

Are you going to ask me, "Why are you exhorting me to practice mental prayer if it is already within me, ready-made and unceasing, and since it is not my business, but that of the Holy Spirit?"

Yes, it is within you like the flame of an oil lamp. But this flame needs to be fed with oil, or it will flicker and go out. The oil that nourishes the prayer of the Spirit within you is your love for God.

By love for God, I do not mean some vague religious emotion or mediocre feeling, but the cleaving of our innermost will to the will and action of the Spirit of the Lord within us.

This adherence varies greatly from one Christian to another. In one individual, it may be implicit, poor and hesitant. In a saint, it is lucid, firm, fervent and inspired by intense faith and charity.

The quality of our prayer is measured by the quality of our adherence to the prayer-activity of the Holy Spirit within us.

It is essential to devote sufficient time to mental prayer because in our everyday life, under the influence of worries, pleasures, and sorrows, our interior adherence to God quickly slackens and declines. When we come to mental prayer, we are in a state of dispersion, like a band of sparrows scattered on trees and in surrounding bushes. We must regroup our faculties and recollect ourselves. That takes time. But then our adherence is made firmer in the measure that our faith intensifies in the presence of God within us, and in the measure that our love for him is actualized.

Perhaps the day will come when there will be no need to devote a specific time to mental prayer. The day will surely come when this profound union with the prayer of the Spirit of Christ within us will remain actual, alive and uninterrupted. Our occupational activities will not disturb it any more. When that happens, the Spirit will carry us along and vivify us, whether we are walking, or working, or talking. Even when we are sleeping—the bride in the Song of Songs cries out, "*I was sleeping, but my heart kept vigil*" (5:2).

That is the unceasing prayer that Christ recommended to his disciples: "*He told them a parable on the necessity of praying always and not losing heart*" (Lk 18:1). St. Paul transmitted the same advice to the Thessalonians: "*Rejoice always, never cease praying, render constant thanks*" (1 Th 5:16-18).

For those who attain to this continual interior mental prayer, the prayer of the Holy Spirit is no longer an ember under the ashes, but a flame that consumes the whole person. A saint is a living prayer.

Now, do you understand what I was saying to you at the beginning of my letter? It is not so much a matter of "practicing" mental prayer, as of "joining yourself" by an act of faith to the prayer of Christ's Spirit within you. You must do this and persist with patience, courage and unshakable hope. One day, I am sure, you will be able to write to me, based on your own personal experience:

"Christ is my life. Not only does he pray with me, but also 'in' and 'through' me. His prayer is my prayer. There are not two prayers side by side, but one prayer which is at once both his and mine."

48. Beloved Father

"God has sent forth into our hearts the Spirit of his Son who cries out 'Abba!' ('Father!')" (Gal 4:6). When we speak of Christian prayer, we must always come back to this verse, from the *Epistle to the Galatians*, which defines its hidden meaning. But we must read it correctly, and not pass over the essential word. The fact that Paul thought it wise to preserve the Aramaic word *abba* in his Greek text deserves attention. He would not have done so, had he thought that the Greek term *pater* was its meticulously exact translation.

He wrote to the Romans, using almost the same words: (You received) *"a spirit of adoption through which we cry out, 'Abba!' (that is, 'Father')"* (Rm 8:15). We find the same word in Mark's Gospel. At the hour of Christ's unimaginable anguish at Gethsemane, this is the word that came to his lips: *"Abba (O Father), you have the power to do all things. Take this cup away from me"* (Mk 14:36).

Some of the greatest exegetes conclude, from the use of this term by Paul and Mark, that the primitive communities preserved this word with great devotion and infinite veneration. These communities had no relics of Christ. They had something much better—the very word that sprang from his heart in his dialogue with God: *Abba!* It was a great delight for these first Christians, when they spoke to the Father, to be able to use the very word of the mother tongue of Christ Jesus.

But this was not only a demand of the heart. They had no term that could express the exact nuance of meaning of the word *abba*, the diminutive that Aramaic speaking children used in addressing their fathers. It was the word that the child Jesus called out to Joseph: *abba,*

abba! To render the nuance of intimate and trusting tenderness contained in this *abba*, we must translate it as "beloved father" or "my dearest father."

Do you understand now why this word was so precious to the primitive Church? The Apostles had been deeply moved when they heard Christ use it to pray to the Lord of heaven and earth (cf. Mk 14:36). What Jew would have dared to invoke God in this way, he whose holiness caused the seraphim and the prophets to tremble? There were times when God was called "our Father" (*abinou* in Hebrew, *abunan* in Aramaic), or more rarely and solemnly "my Father" (*abi*). But never, absolutely never, would anyone have used a term expressing such childlike trust as *abba*.

For Christ, the use of the term *abba* to address God was a way of expressing and affirming his divine Sonship to his friends and followers.

But Christ did not monopolize this filial and trusting familiarity. He taught it to his disciples. In their Gospels, St. Luke and St. Matthew each give us a version of the Lord's Prayer. It is shorter in Luke, and longer and more solemn in Matthew. It is generally thought that Luke gives us the primitive version, the one that Jesus himself taught. It begins in this way: *"Father, hallowed by your name, your kingdom come. Give us each day our daily bread . . ."* (Lk 11:2-3).

Some exegetes think that the first word was *"Abba!* Beloved Father."* Thus, the disciples could address God with filial tenderness, as did their Master. Indeed, this is the great revelation that Jesus Christ brought to the world. Those who believe in him are children of God in a very real, and not a metaphorical, sense. For they are "begotten of God," "born of God," "sharers in his nature."

What an astounding revelation! Whenever the first Christians said to God, "Beloved Father!", their hearts leaped with joy. How is it for us?

To the man or woman who prays to him in this way, God responds, as he does to Jesus: *"You are my beloved Son"* (Mk 1:11; Lk 3:22).

Jesus did more than teach his followers the terms they should use in prayer. Beginning with Pentecost, he sent the Holy Spirit, who murmurs *Abba!* in the depths of every Christian heart. If we knew how to live inwardly, we could not fail to recognize his voice. It seems that St. Paul's correspondents were more keenly attuned to the inspirations of the Spirit than we are. In fact, to remind them that they were sons of

God, the Apostle did not hesitate to write to them (I am slightly paraphrasing his text):

* * *

"When you recollect yourselves, a word, a cry, leaps from the depths of your consciousness: *Abba!* That should not surprise you. You have received the Holy Spirit, the Spirit of the Son. He inspires the sentiments of the Son within you, and brings to your lips the very invocation of Christ: '*Abba*, beloved Father!' What better proof could you want of your divine sonship?"

* * *

Is it because St. Matthew feared that the Christian's filial familiarity might degenerate into impertinence, that he put an adjunct in his version of the Lord's Prayer: "*Our Father in heaven*" (Mt 6:9)? This keeps us from putting God on the same footing as the fathers of earth, forgetting his supreme greatness. But the clarification is not an invitation to moderate our filial trust. It is meant far more to make us aware of a magnificent reality. The holy, eternal, all-powerful God has invited us to address him with the tenderness of a little child: "*Abba*, Dearest Daddy! My beloved Father!"

49. Veni, Come

Y ou ask whether we must pray to the Holy Spirit. Run through your missal. It will give you the answer by way of admirable prayers to the Third Person of the Trinity. Among others, the *Veni Sancte Spiritus (Come, thou Holy Spirit, come!)*, the Sequence of the Mass, and the *Veni Creator (Creator Spirit, come)*. The *Veni Creator* is the hymn that the Church invites us to sing on solemn occasions, such as the opening of great church assemblies.

You probably know the other *Veni Sancte Spiritus (Come, Holy Spirit)*. I, for one, recited it thousands of times in school—before our noisy English classes and before our mortally boring math classes. I hate myself for not even suspecting the richness of the words I was pronouncing.

Veni, Come. That is how these prayers begin. Their first word is addressed to the One whose presence we desire within us. And it is indeed God's will that the Holy Spirit be our guest, that we be his temple (cf. Rm 8:9; 1 Cor 3:16; 1 Cor 6:19).

Prayers addressed specifically to the Person of the Holy Spirit are less frequent in our Latin liturgy than they are in the East. But what do our prayers to Christ and to the Father ask basically, if not the gift of the Holy Spirit? It is the object of the divine promises throughout the history of the people of God. Is not all prayer ordered to our sanctification? Now, it is the Holy Spirit who makes sons and daughters of God out of us. He fashions within us filial souls, from which rise the cry of tenderness and trust: *"Abba! Father!"* (cf. Rm 8:14-15).

In our prayer to the Holy Spirit, we cry out to him: *Veni*. When we address Christ or the Father, we ask of them: *Emitte*. Send the Holy Spirit. Send to us, send within us, the Spirit who alone can re-form us, according to Ezekiel's admirable prophecy: *"I will give you a new heart and place a new spirit within you, taking from your bodies your stony hearts and giving you natural hearts. I will put my Spirit within you and make you live by my statutes"* (Ezk 36:26-27).

Not only every individual person, but the entire universe will be renewed by his coming. A short verse from the liturgy of Pentecost expresses it splendidly: *"Send forth your Spirit, and all things will be created. And you shall renew the face of the earth."*

Do I need to insist any more, to convince you that you ought to pray to the Holy Spirit?

I wonder whether the difficulty you have in praying to him does not stem from the fact that you seek him as someone exterior to yourself, when he is right there inside of you. He is not holding a dialogue with you from outside yourself. He is a living spring welling up within you that inspires, sustains, and encourages your prayer, your faith and your love.

This was well grasped by the little girl whose mother was arranging her white veil for her confirmation. "Mother," she said, "I think I've already received him." "Who did you receive, dear?" "The Holy Spirit." "What makes you think so?" "I always feel like doing good things."

The Spirit instructs us in the secret dwelling within us, in our innermost soul where he resides. He teaches not with words, but by infusing his knowledge into us. That is the way we must understand

Christ's promise: *"The Paraclete, the Holy Spirit . . . will instruct you in everything, and remind you of all that I told you"* (Jn 14:26).

The Holy Spirit teaches us to pray, not by proposing formulas of prayer to us, but by making prayer well up within us as a cry to God.

As our friend, the Holy Spirit consoles us, but not after the manner of earthly friends. His help comes from within. He is the energy that strengthens our will, and the fire that brings our heart to incandescence. "Kindle in our hearts the fire of your love."

We can expect from the Holy Spirit nothing less than our complete interior renewal. The litany of petitions in the Sequence of Pentecost is remarkably expressive: *"Wash . . . rectify . . . heal . . . bend . . . warm . . . guide and redress. . . ."* At the center of our being, he is truly the Spirit who creates and re-creates.

Why, then, are we so meagerly transformed by him? Because he has infinite respect for our freedom, and refuses to make a forced entry into our souls. He will not come to our help unless we cleave to him. The Holy Spirit is all-powerful only in the person who consents to be poor, attentive, docile, ductile, tractable, flexible and manageable. With such a person, he accomplishes great things. But we have to receive these very qualities as gifts from him: "Make me docile and then teach me, make me tractable and then lead me."

The Apostles received the Holy Spirit only because, united in heart and mind, they persevered in prayer together with a few women including Mary, the Mother of Jesus (cf. Ac 1:14), in expectation of his coming. It is up to you to make each of your times of mental prayer a new Pentecost.

"Hallowed be your name!" (Mt 6:9)

In the Christian's prayer, we find the various elements that make up the prayer of the Son of God who became man.

The first reaction of anyone who places himself in the presence of God (of his excellence, his splendor and his holiness) is a sense of reverential awe. It is a sentiment akin not to fear but to an adoring love.

50   *Remember Bichr*—To adore is to confess: "You alone are God," in an interior attitude of awe and love, wonder and joy.

51   *"You shall do homage to the Lord your God"* (Mt 4:10)—Praise springs from adoration. The prostrate man rises to his feet to celebrate the perfections and great works of his God.

52   *"To praise his glory"* (Ep 1:12)—To give him thanks for his help and his munificence, and above all to thank him for all that HE IS.

53   *Thanks for being you*—These varied attitudes culminate in an extremely rich spiritual perspective that encompasses and overflows them. This is the self-offering of oneself in a "sacrifice of praise."

54   *At Ronchamp*—In this offering, the Christian commits his whole being: his past, present and future, his body and soul, his life and death.

55   *Letter to Jean Pierre*—But, by contrast with inanimate objects, man does not offer himself up once and for all. Only the person who never ceases offering himself or herself to God, is truly given to God.

56   *Second letter to Jean Pierre*—Our offering of love is a repayment to the Lord for the superabundant life that his love has given us.

57   *Third letter to Jean Pierre*—At a deeper level, it is a participation in the surge of thanksgiving that has impelled the Son into the arms of the Father from all eternity.

58   *Fourth letter to Jean Pierre*—In the saints, this need to offer oneself to God becomes a desire for self-abasement. This desire must be

rightly understood. It is a vehement yearning to be consumed by divine love, the way that sacrifices of ancient times were consumed by the fire that fell from heaven.

50. Remember Bichr

I t gives me great joy to know that you need only hear the name of God spoken, or see it written, to experience deep within your soul a mysterious movement of adoration. It is proof that the virtue of religion is alive within you. This is the spiritual inclination to honor and revere God, and to work for his glory. But you should also realize that it is an invitation to diligently cultivate this virtue, which is the foundation of all religions. This is so true, that religions are designated by the very word that serves to denote this virtue.

There is a close bond between the virtue of religion, and love. Who was it who said, "To love is to honor"? This is already true in our human relations. All the more is it true in our relations with God. True love for God is impatient to acknowledge his supreme excellence, and to proclaim it so that every creature may render him honor and glory.

Some Christians, of course, use the pretext of filial love to explain the fact that, when they are in the presence of God, they do not experience the reverential awe that the virtue of religion begets. They treat God with a familiarity that borders on insolence. You can be sure that, far from having exceeded the "law of fear" as they imagine, they have not even begun to be religious.

Be an assiduous reader of the Old Testament, especially of the prophets, those champions of the transcendent holiness of God. Their words have extraordinary power to bring forth the virtue of religion (which the Old Testament calls the "fear of God") and make it grow and ripen. You will discover that simultaneously there will develop within you an ever bolder filial trust. Indeed, the more a Christian "fears" God, the more he loves him. And the more he loves him, the more he "fears" him. This only seems to be a paradox.

I want to leave you with an anecdote, which for centuries has taught young Moslems to respect the Name. I am sure you will sense its profoundly religious tone:

* * *

"One night, Bichr the barefoot tramp was wandering about in a drunken stupor. He happened to find a piece of paper on the ground, already trampled on by the feet of many passers-by. On it was written: 'In the name of God, the clement, the merciful. . . .' He picked up the piece of paper and wrapped it in a bit of cloth, attaching to it a tiny parcel of musk, and respectfully placed the little packet in the cleft in an old wall.

"That same night a devout personage of the city had a dream, in which he was commanded to go and tell Bichr: 'Since you have picked up our Name that was lying on the ground, since you cleaned it and perfumed it, we, too, shall honor your name in this world and in the next.' "

51. *"You shall do homage to the Lord your God"* (Mt 4:10)

First of all, here is an excerpt from the letter to which my own letter is an answer:

* * *

"I love to adore. I feel impelled to adore. I am happy when I adore God and I should even say that I am never so happy as when I am adoring. And yet I must add that I don't know what adoration is. Isn't that paradoxical? I have often searched in books, inspired by the hope that at last I was about to find the definition of this adoration which holds first place in my life. Each time, I have been disappointed by the diversity of definitions or descriptions. Adoration is presented as man's reaction to the presence of God's sovereignty, or of his majesty or glory. It is described by some as the presentiment of his terrifying proximity. For others, it is the spiritual attitude of man confronting the Being who is his origin and his end. From this it follows that adoration of God is compared, depending on the circumstances, to reverential fear or to praise, to submission or to homage. Isn't that playing games with adoration? If it is not defined rigorously, it dissolves into diverse religious attitudes, and loses its specificity. For me, this is a very serious matter."

* * *

Dear friend, I am happy to hear you say that you are deeply drawn to adoration. It is the indubitable sign of the presence of the Spirit of God within you. It shows that your religion is not simply the moralism or the vague religiousness that so many Christians mistake for true religion. We cannot help wondering whether such Christians are atheists without knowing it.

In order to grasp what authentic adoration is, start out from the affirmations of Scripture: *"You shall do homage to the Lord your God; him alone shall you adore"* (Mt 4:10). This commandment had for centuries been the fundamental rule for the Jewish people. Christ solemnly proclaimed it anew at the dawn of the Messianic era (cf. Lk 4:8). And he added: *"Yet an hour is coming, and is already here, when authentic worshippers will worship the Father in Spirit and truth. . . . God is Spirit, and those who worship him must worship in Spirit and truth"* (Jn 4:23-24).

Isn't it clear from these texts that adoration is an act of man that can be addressed only to God? The first Christians understood it in this way, and they died by the thousands for refusing to worship emperors or idols.

The other religious attitudes—reverence, praise, love—by contrast with adoration, are to be found also in human relations. Indeed, God does not claim to be the only one to be revered, praised, and loved. But he does not tolerate that men should adore anyone other than him: *"The Lord is 'the Jealous One', a jealous God is he"* (Ex 34:14).

Clearly, adoration is addressed to God *simply because he is God.* Adoration is that deep-seated attitude of soul (whether or not it is translated by external gestures or activities) that proclaims: "There is a God. You are God. You alone are God." Therefore, the object of adoration is not one or another of God's perfections, but the Godhead as Godhead, independently of his attributes.

Granted, when I affirm through adoration that the One before whom I stand is God, I am by that very fact acknowledging his admirable perfections. And these perfections (his oneness, simplicity, truth, goodness, infinity, eternity, incomprehensibility, wisdom, providence, justice, mercy and omnipotence) inspire the multifarious religious sentiments: fear, admiration, reverence, obedience, praise, repentance, thanksgiving, trust and filial love. But these sentiments, which are the escort of adoration, are not adoration. It should even be added that without adoration, all these sentiments would be nothing. For they derive all their religious value from adoration.

However, it is equally true that adoration attains its plenitude only by incorporating these diverse sentiments, and being nourished by their substance. Only then does it appear in its splendor as filial adoration, trusting and jubilant.

The unspoken adoration of man, who is not a pure spirit, expresses itself through corporeal attitudes, of which prostrating himself is unquestionably the most characteristic. There are so many pages of the Bible on which we read: *"They prostrated themselves and worshipped him"* (cf. 2 M 3:15; Mt 2:11; etc.). It also finds expression in divine worship, *latria*, reserved for God alone. Its privileged manifestation is sacrifice.

Even so, the adorer in spirit and in truth always remembers that external worship is empty of meaning, unless it is rooted in interior worship. Christ flung at the Pharisees the reprimand that Isaiah the prophet had hurled at his contemporaries in the name of Yahweh: *"This people pays me lip service but their heart is far from me. They do me empty reverence, making dogmas out of human precepts"* (Mt 15:8-9; Is 29:13).

Because man is a social being, he is inclined to translate his adoration and worship into social terms. That is, he confesses his gratitude to God publicly, and joins in with other men: "Come, let us adore him...."

In the last analysis, you will have a complete understanding of adoration only if you consider it in the life of the great Adorer, Jesus Christ. Indeed, as the perfect man, endowed with a created human nature, his first religious obligation was adoration of the Father. This was the warp and woof of his earthly life, in the carpenter shop at Nazareth as well as on the roads of Palestine. It was in the sacrifice of Calvary that Christ's adoration attained its supreme expression. It was on the Cross that Jesus proclaimed to the whole world that there is only one God, and that this God (whose love went to the extreme limit of giving his own Son) insists on being adored by all creatures.

The great uninterrupted adoration which rises *"from the rising sun to the setting sun"* (cf. Ba 5:5) from all the sons and daughters of God, is the same as the firstborn Son's adoration. He himself transfuses it into the heart of each of his brothers and sisters.

52. *"To praise his glory"* (Ep 1:12)

D ear friend, I wonder if you are giving sufficient room to praise in your prayer?

Do you perhaps have doubts about the value that God attributes to praise? In that case, leaf through the Psalter and you will find praise on almost every page. Now, the Psalter is the book which the Lord himself has given us, to teach us how to pray.

But at the same time, you will also come to understand that the source of praise is the knowledge of God. The fervent Jews were men of praise only because they were first of all "seekers after God." We do not sing hymns of praise to something or someone we know nothing about!

They loved to contemplate the wondrous works of the Lord. Listen to their acclamations:

* * *

> *"O Lord, our Lord,*
> *how glorious is your name over all*
> *the earth!"*   (Ps 8:2)
> *"For you make me glad O Lord,*
> *by your deeds;*
> *at the works of your hands I rejoice."*
>
>   (Ps 92:5)

* * *

They meditated a long time on what they called the "mighty deeds" of the One who had delivered them *"with his strong hand and outstretched arm"* (Dt 5:15):

* * *

> *"Give thanks to the Lord, invoke his*
> *name;*
> *make known among the nations his deeds. . . .*
> *Glory in his holy name;*
> *rejoice, O hearts that seek the Lord!"*
>
>   (Ps 105:1, 3)

* * *

But they were filled with wonder at the perfections of God even more than at his works. They marveled at God's holiness, glory, power and unfathomable love. This love is the wellspring of all his works and of all his divine interventions:

* * *

> *"Give thanks to the Lord for he is good,*
> *for his mercy endures forever; . . .*
> *Who alone does great wonders,*
> *for his mercy endures forever!"*

(Ps 136:1, 4)

* * *

Even before it becomes words on men's lips, praise is a silent exultation, an ovation to God deep within the heart. Like a spreading fire, it gradually engulfs the whole of man's being. Then it bursts forth in jubilant hymns. Then a King David, laughing at protocol, begins to dance around the Ark. The believer becomes a "living praise."

And this praise is no longer reserved for feast days, but is a basic, never-ceasing prayer:

* * *

> *"I will bless the Lord at all times;*
> *his praise shall be ever in my mouth."* (Ps 34:2)
> *"That my soul might sing praise to you*
> *without ceasing;*
> *O Lord, my God, forever will I give*
> *you thanks."* (Ps 30:13)

* * *

And when praise is on the verge of growing weary, the believer exhorts himself:

* * *

"Praise the Lord, O my soul;
I will praise the Lord all my life;
I will sing praise to my God while I live."

(Ps 146:1-2)

* * *

But make no mistake about it. The man of praise is neither an individualist nor a dilettante. He cannot admire without joining his brothers to himself, to worthily celebrate the object of his admiration. That is why he cannot refrain from convoking all the members of the People of God to praise:

* * *

"You who fear the Lord, praise him;
all you descendants of Jacob, give glory to him!"

(Ps 22:24)

* * *

On a broader scale, forgetting his national particularism, he addresses his invitation to all peoples;

* * *

"Praise the Lord, all you nations;
glorify him, all you peoples!"

(Ps 117:1)

* * *

Even inanimate creatures are necessary for the worship of praise:

* * *

"Let the heavens be glad and the earth
rejoice;

let the sea and what fills it resound;
let the plains be joyful. . . ."
"Let the rivers clap their hands,
and the mountains shout with them for joy!"

(Ps 96:11-12; 98:8)

* * *

How can Christians, for whom God has done so much more, and revealed unheard-of secrets of love, fail to be men of praise as well?

The reasons for praise that inspired the Psalmist's hymns are not foreign to Christians, as the considerable place allotted to the ancient Psalms of Israel in the liturgy demonstrates. But Christians have a loftier motive that inspires them to a loftier praise. This is the celebration of the fatherhood of God, the exultant acclamation of his paternal tenderness. For they know what the Jews did not know:

* * *

"Yes, God so loved the world that he gave his only Son, that whoever believes in him may not die, but may have eternal life" (Jn 3:16).

* * *

And this eternal life is not some ordinary, commonplace grace, but an unimaginable reality:

* * *

"See what love the Father has bestowed on us in letting us be called children of God! Yet that is what we are"1 (1 Jn 3:1).

★ ★ ★

There are many Christians who, because they do not truly believe that they are sons and heirs of God (cf. Gal 4:7), languish in the mediocrity of anxiety. When they approach their Lord in prayer, more often than not it is to beg for some favor, rather than to give thanks.

When one is with them, one scarcely has the impression of being in the presence of *"a people God has made his own, to praise his glory"* (Ep 1:14).

Fortunately, there are Christians who understand their vocation of praise. This praise has great value in the eyes of God, for he discerns in it the accents of his Son's prayer. To make this truth clear, certain Fathers of the Church liked to compare Christ to King David, who celebrated the Lord to the accompaniment of musical instruments. But, they add, the new David shuns the lyre and the zither, instruments devoid of soul. To praise his Father, Christ uses the accompaniment of the intelligent and free instrument that is man, composed of body and soul. Thus, in and through the Christian who praises his God, it is Christ himself who expresses his eternal and joyous thanksgiving to his beloved Father.

The praise of the Christian is Christ's own praise.

The praise of the Church is the praise of the total Christ, present throughout the world.

53. Thanks for being you

I can't remember where I read that Father Charles de Foucauld experienced immense joy in singing to God this verse of the *Gloria*: *"we give you thanks, we praise you for your glory!"*

We Christians of every denomination give thanks to God for his gifts, his help and his munificence. And too often, like the nine lepers in the Gospel, we forget to say even a plain and simple Thank-you!

Where the saints are concerned, it is the splendor of God, his infinite majesty, and immeasurable goodness that release the well-springs of thanksgiving in their hearts. They are filled with wonder and satisfaction, not so much by what God gives them, as by what God is. Even if they were to receive nothing from him, their praise would be no less fervent and their happiness no less ecstatic.

This is surely one of the most delicate, most refined, and rarest sentiments (in the twofold sense of being infrequent and of great value). There are persons so totally unconcerned with themselves, who have so completely overcome every instinct of possessiveness, that they do not need to receive a favor in order to be filled with gratitude. For them, it suffices that something beautiful *exists*.*

Such an attitude of soul requires a long apprenticeship of unalloyed love and renunciation. And yet it is sometimes seen burgeoning in the heart of a child, like the early primrose that anticipates the coming of Spring.

I am reminded of a little girl who was close to appreciating and adopting the verse of the *Gloria*. Her mother told me that the child had said to her, "Thanks, Mommy." "Thanks for what, dear?" "For being YOU."

54. At Ronchamp

A student came and told me how he had discovered mental prayer. I'll tell you his story. Perhaps it will help you to pray better.

It was at Ronchamp in the church built by Le Corbusier, a unique monument. It is a true creation—something one is rarely tempted to think when viewing a work of art. Deep inside the church on the Epistle side, there is a chapel. Imagine a round tower, 13 feet in diameter and 50 feet high (approximate figures). There is total denudation. The walls are covered with a grayish-white roughcast, uneven and rugged, and unrelieved by any decoration whatsoever. Light comes from above, but the openings through which it enters are invisible. Below, there is semidarkness. Even so, when the eyes gradually turn upward they encounter the intense light of the top of the tower. A diver might well have a similar sensation when he looks up to the surface of the water from a distance of several fathoms below.

In this chapel, more naked than a monk's cell, there is only one object. In the middle, facing you, is an altar made of a large block of stone, devoid of ornamentation and with nothing at all upon it.** The upper surface is slightly larger than the lower one, which gives a sense of upward motion.

* *Translator's note*: Ralph Waldo Emerson expressed a similar thought: "Never lose an opportunity of seeing anything that is beautiful, for beauty is God's handwriting—a wayside sacrament. Welcome it in every fair face, in every fair sky, in every flower, and thank God for it as a cup of blessing."

** Regretfully, since that time a crucifix and sconces have been placed on the altar. The impression one gets is altogether different now.

Well, my young friend was there, deeply moved by the pervading sense of recollection. In this translucid atmosphere, in this denuded place in which there was nothing to tantalize the imagination, the emotions, or the intellect, he sensed an irresistible invitation emanating from the bare altar. An altar is meant to hold something. It is the table of God, the place where man presents his offerings, where God accepts and consecrates them.

In this poor cell, my friend saw nothing he could present on the altar, except himself. He suddenly understood that God was asking him to offer himself—his intellect, heart, body and liberty—in an act of adoration.

Since that day, when my friend begins his mental prayer he often thinks of that altar waiting for something, waiting for him. And he offers himself. He reflects that the victim on the altar has nothing better to do than to remain there at God's service, as though drawn up by the light from above. His active mental prayer consists in maintaining his soul in this attitude of offering, absorbed in God, beseeching him to accept his "sacrifice of praise."

55. Letter to Jean Pierre

I agree that there is an ever-present danger that our mental prayer may be reduced to a superficial activity that does not commit our innermost self. You are right to dread such a thing.

I am inclined to think that for quite a few people, mental prayer is simply the gentle purring of a cat in front of a fire. For others, it is a torrent of words devoid of substance. The latter deserve Christ's reprimand: *"None of those who cry out, 'Lord, Lord,' will enter the kingdom of God but only the one who does the will of my Father in heaven"* (Mt 7:21).

The truth is, that we can talk to God without committing ourselves to him. We can engage in subtle meditations, experience great spiritual emotions, and still not commit ourselves.

What interior act during mental prayer will involve you deeply, make you commit yourself, and make you surrender your past as well as your future to God? What act will make you put your life on the line? One word describes this act: *self-offering*. Yes, mental prayer is first of all the offering of ourselves to God.

Perhaps you will ask me, "Why don't you speak instead of loving?"

Actually, loving and offering oneself are not separable. Self-offering is to love, what fruit is to the tree. The patient, secret labor of the tree during the long winter prepares the delectable fruit that the June sun ripens on the branch. The same is true of self-offering, the fruit of love patiently developed during many periods of prayer. One day during mental prayer, it falls off of its own weight into God's hand, as he reaches out to pick it.

St. Paul has a wonderfully powerful sentence to invite us to this self-offering. I would like you to know it by heart, to repeat it slowly and with great attention at the beginning of your mental prayer: *"And now, brothers, I beg you through the mercy of God to offer your bodies as a living sacrifice holy and acceptable to God, your spiritual worship"* (Rm 12:1). Is there a better definition of mental prayer?

56. Second Letter to Jean Pierre

I was not expecting the strange conclusion you drew from my last letter. "If mental prayer consists essentially in offering oneself, I don't see why you ask me to practice mental prayer every day. Once this offering has been made, in truth and totally, with full knowledge and consent, what's the use of renewing it daily? What's done is done." In reading your letter, I was reminded of what a husband told his young wife, who had just chided him for never expressing his love: "Come now, you wouldn't want to make me look ridiculous by repeating to you every day what I told you once and for all!"

"What's done is done." Your assertion is less logical than it appears to be. A person does not give himself like an inanimate object. When you have given your watch or your pen, that's it. There's no use thinking about it any more. But a living person is given only to the degree that he maintains and perseveres in the act of self-giving. As soon as he departs from this basic attitude of mind, he is no longer given. It's true of human love, and it's true with God.

It is therefore of utmost importance to acquire the *habitual* attitude of self-offering to God. Once it has been acquired, you must defend and nurture it or it will soon lose its vigor and its truth. Now, the privileged means of acquiring, defending, and nurturing this attitude is mental prayer. Only mental prayer helps us to advance toward the permanent gift of self to God. Only mental prayer renews and energizes its dynamism. Mental prayer is the most vital time of a life offered to God.

57. Third Letter to Jean Pierre

To practice mental prayer is to offer oneself to the Lord, as I was telling you in my two last letters. But what is this impetus that impels the Christian to offer himself to his God? There are several constituent elements, but one of them takes precedence over all the rest, and gives self-offering its hallmark: gratitude.

When you come before God, and think about him, you cannot help being impressed by his generosity. He has heaped his gifts upon you, and he never stops. If your heart is in the right place, your gratitude wells up spontaneously to your God. In response to his love that gives, your love acknowledges him and gives thanks.

And if you meditate in greater depth, you soon understand what distinguishes God from other benefactors. They offer you gifts that increase your *possessions*. God, for his part, never stops giving you a more fundamental gift: your *existence*. You become aware that if he interrupted his action, you would immediately sink back into nothingness. And so, gratitude thrills in you once more. But this time, it is more than an intense and impassioned sentiment. It is like a return of your whole being toward God. Suddenly, the river flows back towards its source.

Your meditation has still greater things to discover. God does not only give you your being, your natural life. He also gives you your supernatural life, the one whose seed he implanted in you through baptism, and which he never stops cultivating through his sacraments. When you really become aware of this prodigious gift—God communicating his own life to you—you rush, swept along by grace, toward him in gratitude and joyfully offer yourself to his tender paternal embrace.

So you see that gratitude has welled up at every stage of your meditation. It is the underlying dynamism that inspires the man of prayer to offer himself to God.

Now, let us call it by its Christian name: *thanksgiving*. In response to God's love which is grace, man's love wells up in thanksgiving. Grace and thanksgiving are the two poles of the dialogue of love between God and man.

Thanksgiving is certainly much more than a matter of words and feelings. It is the joyous, loving gift of self, irrevocable and without reservation.

58. Fourth Letter to Jean Pierre

H ave I succeeded in making you realize that thanksgiving, the soul of mental prayer, is something very different from a superficial sentiment? It is the surging up of our innermost self which, having come forth from God, returns to God. It is the ebb and flow of love. God's love is poured out on his child, and a filial love leaps back toward the Father. One and the same love comes forth from God and returns to him, a paternal love at the start, and a filial love when it returns.

This exchange of love between God and man reflects—and is part of—a much loftier reality: the love between the Father and the Son within the Trinity. From all eternity, the Father, in a surge of divine generosity, has communicated the fullness of his being, without reservation or intermittence, to his beloved Son. From all eternity, the Son has received the Father's gift, and offered himself to him in a joyous leap of thanksgiving. This love that gives and this love that renders thanks are, as it were, "two powerful waves that impetuously rush toward one another, meet, meld into one, and leap up together from their bed in an immense geyser" (Richard of Saint-Victor).

The Son of God has come into our midst to celebrate his eternal thanksgiving within a human nature. In the heart of the man Jesus, the unimaginable Trinitarian mystery is being lived. The Son surrenders himself totally to the Father who is giving himself to him. *"Father, I thank you . . . "* (Jn 11:41, etc.). This little prayer, which rises so often from Jesus' lips, is very revealing of his innermost life, of his eternal religion, incarnated in his humanity.

The thanksgiving of Jesus was manifested in all its plenitude and power at the Passion and the Resurrection. Triumphing over suffering and death, it carried him up in a conquering flight to the right hand of the Father.

Even so, Christ has never stopped celebrating here on earth the great liturgy of thanksgiving. Day after day, hour after hour, from the rising to the setting sun, the Mass has perpetuated over the centuries the act by which Jesus offered himself in thanksgiving to the Father, in his own name and in the name of the human race.

But Christ's love aspires to still greater things. To give thanks for and among all men is not enough for him. He wants millions of hearts and millions of voices. He takes possession of these hearts through Eucharistic Communion. He implants in them his own eternal thanksgiving to germinate and develop, so that it may be celebrated not only in church, but may also be lived in all times and places by all who open their hearts and souls to it.

As for mental prayer, it is that privileged hour when all occupations come to a halt, and the Christian devotes himself unreservedly to Christ's own thanksgiving.

"*Assembled in Unity*"

In Christ who has taken possession of him, the Christian is united to all his brothers and sisters, in heaven and on earth. Their spiritual riches belong to him, and his belong to them. Together with them, he accepts responsibility for all those who do not yet know their heavenly Father.

It is only in the Church, the gathering of the Lord's children assembled in prayer, that we can encounter God and pray to him. There, everyone prays in the name of all, and all pray in the name of each.

59 *Shoulder to shoulder*—During mental prayer, we have available to us much more than our own individual resources. We have the inexhaustible love and prayers of all the members of God's family.

60 *The organist's little daughter*—At the hour of prayer, we must unite not only with the Church of this earth, but also with the Church of heaven, with the great heavenly liturgy of the angels and saints.

61 *Jacobs's ladder*—And at the center of the great assembly of all of God's children, behold Mary, our Mother, who melds our prayer into her prayer!

62 and 63 *The presence of Mary*—To rally the Church to prayer does not mean that we are turning away from the multitudes who don't know the Lord, or who reject him. How could we glimpse the splendor, the sovereignty and the Fatherhood of God without feeling the need to make them known to others?

64 *Atheism and mental prayer*—The man of prayer, by his silent presence, is already doing the Lord's work, which is to *"gather into one all the dispersed children of God"* (Jn 11:52).

65 *Black Mimoûna*—In addition, he intercedes for the world, so that it may be preserved from the punishments that men's innumerable sins call down loudly upon it.

66 *"In the breach"*—To intercede is much more than simply to plead the cause of one's brothers. It is to be eager to inaugurate God's reign, and to allow his all-powerful love to pass freely through oneself.

67 *With outstretched arms*—Through prayer, man collaborates in God's work, not only within himself but also in the entire world.

68 *To pray is to cooperate with God.*

59. Shoulder to shoulder

I f we want to find God, we must go to the place where he is waiting for us. For he has chosen certain meeting-places. For the Hebrews, during their long sojourn in the desert, it was "the Tent of Meeting." After their settlement in Canaan, it was Jerusalem, and within Jerusalem, the Temple. Sacrifices were not to be offered anywhere else. The Temple was the "House of God," also called the "House of prayer" by the prophets. The prayers that each individual offered in his home or in the synagogue were directed toward the Temple. Thus, the prophet Daniel always kept open the window of his upper room that faced towards the Holy City.

But the Temple was only an image, an anticipation of the definitive house of God that is the Church, the great gathering of all the faithful of earth and heaven. The Church is indeed the "Holy Temple," as St. Paul says, "the spiritual dwelling," the new House of prayer.

Whenever we want to pray, we must go to the House of God, we must enter *into the Church*. By this, I mean that we must become aware once more of belonging to the Church. Any one of us who isolates himself will never encounter God, because it is within the Church, the Mystical Body of his Son, that he awaits us. "Outside the Church there is no salvation" because outside of Christ, outside God's family, outside the House of God, we have no way of finding God.*

I fear that you are experiencing the temptation of spiritual individualism. This may be the explanation for your bouts with discouragement. I invite you to pray within the Church, spiritually united to all your brothers and sisters.

---

* We should not conclude from this, that the prayers of non-Christians are devoid of value. But it is through the Church, which assumes and offers them, that they find their way to God.

Pray *in the midst of them*, join your voice to the prayers of the priests and the faithful, of the men of yesterday, today, and tomorrow.

Pray also *in their name*. Consider yourself deputed to pray. Lend your voice, your soul, to the entire community which wants to address itself to the Father through you. Did not Christ invite us to say: "*Our Father . . . give us . . .*"? The Christian should not pray only in his own name, or petition only for himself.

And that is not all. You must also pray *through* all your brothers and sisters. Know that in the great fraternal communion they are at your service. Claudel has expressed it in his inimitable way in *Un Poète regarde la Croix* (A Poet Looks at the Cross). Listen to what he has to say:

* * *

"We have much more than our own faculties to love, understand and serve God. We have everything available to us all at once, from the Blessed Virgin Mary at the summit of the heavens, to the miserable African leper who, holding a bell in his hand, exhales the responses of the Mass through his half-rotted lips. The whole of the visible and invisible creation, the whole of history, the past, the present, and the future, the whole of nature, all the riches of the saints multiplied by grace; all, absolutely all of this is at our service. It is an extension of ourselves, to be used for noble purposes.

"All the saints, all the angels belong to us. We can use the intellect of St. Thomas, the arm of St. Michael, the hearts of Joan of Arc and Catherine of Siena, and all those latent resources that we have only to touch to make them overflow. It is as if everything good, great and beautiful that is done from one end of the earth to the other, everything that holiness accomplishes, were our own doing. It is as if the heroism of the missionaries, the inspiration of the doctors, the generosity of the martyrs, the genius of the artists, the spirited prayer of the Poor Clares and the Carmelites, were all in ourselves. In fact they are us! From the North to the South, from Alpha to Omega, from the East to the West, all things are one with us. We are clothed with all of this and we set all of this into motion."

* * *

Play the game honestly and generously. Never begin your mental prayer without uniting yourself to the "total Christ," to the multitude of believers in adoration before the Father. Always feel that you are shoulder to shoulder with your brothers and sisters everywhere.

And then pray with them, through them and for them. Very often you will be surprised to discover that you are rich and strong, although you had come to prayer overwhelmed with your weakness, your poverty, and your solitude.

60. The organist's little daughter

One evening when I was having dinner with Maurice and his family, he was indignant when he heard me allude to the cult of the saints. I asked him what he meant, and he explained. During a day of recollection with a few of his classmates, the preacher advised them to leave devotion to the saints to the old women.

Maurice was a "neat" fellow, sixteen years old, quick as a whip, straight as an arrow, intelligent and aggressive. As I was leaving, he asked me to write down the answer I had given him, and he added, "I'll read your letter to my pals."

A few days later, I sent him the letter I am now sending you. It was the start of a correspondence that made me discover in him an unexpected spiritual maturity. Our correspondence was brutally ended six months later, by Maurice's accidental death.

* * *

My dear Maurice, you were very much surprised the other evening, when I admitted that I liked to pray to the saints. You wondered if you were talking with a survivor from the "dark ages." I am not willing to lose your esteem, so I am defending myself.

First of all, allow me to give you some advice. I hope that you will hold it as precious as the explorer holds his compass when he is traveling through the wilderness. When you hear anyone express an idea, or when an idea comes to your mind, that appears to contradict a venerable, indisputable, and essential tradition of the Church, always begin by giving the benefit of the doubt to the tradition.

Now, that applies to the present matter. The cult of the saints has been held in great honor by the Church for nearly two thousand years. Almost every day, the liturgy celebrates one or another of these saints. Once a year, all the saints are honored together. And in the most solemn ceremonies—for example, the ordination of priests—the Litany of the Saints is sung, asking them to pray for us.

How can anyone have told you that belief in the intercession of the saints had no Biblical foundation? Peruse the Gospel, and you will see that very often miracles are granted in response to an intercession. The centurion intervenes with Christ for his sick servant, a mother importunes the Lord to cure her little daughter. Why would those whom the Lord has called to himself lose their power of intercession? Why would the Woman who obtained her Son's first miracle at Cana, be less successful in obtaining her requests today?

On his return from the Algerian War, where he had lived through several terrible weeks, I asked one of my friends: "Did you find help in prayer?" He answered:

* * *

"Yes. Not in my own prayer, but in the prayers of my family. There were days when, in a state of physical and nervous exhaustion, shattered to the roots of my being, I was incapable of the slightest prayer. At such times, I remembered my father's last words to me on the platform of the station as I was leaving Lille: 'If there are times when you cannot make yourself pray, remember that the prayers of all of us are with you, and simply say to God: *Lord, I can't pray any more, but listen to the family assembled this evening for their prayer in common.*'"

* * *

Maurice, do you really find it hard to admit that this prayer for a son, a beloved brother, who was far away living through a kind of hell, was powerful before God?

Pity anyone who does not have a family of whom he can think: "At least they are all praying for me!" That is the most hopeless solitude.

But not a single Christian suffers this disgrace. The Church is the family that prays for all the children of God. Not one is excluded from God's thoughts and solicitude. And when I speak of the Church, I evoke both the Church of heaven and the Church of this earth. It is a great error to depend only on our own prayers, and to neglect the prayers of the family!

Are you going to say, "In your view the Church plays the role that rightly belongs to Christ. What need have I of any prayer except his?" You are correct. Christ is the great intercessor. The Epistle to the Hebrews presents him to us as *living forever to make intercession for us* (cf. Heb 7:25). And his intercession suffices. The Father listens only to his prayer. But that's the point! What is the prayer of the Church if not the prayer of Jesus Christ? You believe St. Paul when he declares: *"The life I live now is not my own; Christ is living in me"* (Gal 2:20). Why would it be hard for you to think that it is Jesus Christ who prays in Paul, in Peter and in all my brothers and sisters, when they intercede on my behalf?

"A comparison is not a reason." Even so, I want to leave you with a mental picture. It is a memory from long ago. I was visiting one of our famous French cathedrals under the guidance of the cathedral's organist, who was accompanied by his little six-year-old daughter. After inviting me to admire the portals, the capitals and the stained glass windows, he led me toward the great organs of the cathedral. His daughter Mireille made a request of him, which he at first pretended not to hear. At last he gave in, and started the organ's motor. The child, sitting on the organist's seat with a serious look on her face, struck a chord. And all at once, the ancient stone saints—patriarchs, prophets, martyrs, virgins—came awake. The cathedral vibrated from its foundations to the tip of its slender spire.

Now the delighted child had much more than her own small voice with which to pray to her God. She had at her disposal the immense choir of all the saints she had awakened, the powerful voice of the ancient cathedral, suddenly delivered from its silence. Maurice, it's up to you. It's up to your faith to get all of God's children to start interceding for you—all the saints in heaven, whether famous or unknown and all your brothers and sisters in the Church, whether virtuous or sinful.

This is the law of the communion of saints. Each one is at the service of all, and each one knows he can depend on all the others. St. John of the Cross expressed it very well:

Mine are the heavens, and mine is the earth, and mine are the peoples; the just are mine, and the sinners, too; the angels are mine, and the Mother of God is mine, and all things; even God himself is mine and for me, because Christ is mine and entirely for me.

61. Jacob's ladder

My dear François, I am happy to hear you say that you never pray in isolation, but that, from the beginning of your mental prayer, you join in spirit with your brothers and sisters all over the world. Indeed, a Christian is no longer a solitary person. By his baptism, the great Catholic (i.e., Universal) Assembly is opened to him. When he prays, it must henceforth be *in* the Church, *with* the Church, and *in the name* of the World.

But you must also unite with the heavenly Jerusalem, and not only with the earthly Church. Come now, cross the threshold of the City of God, and enter. A festive assembly will welcome you, the assembly of the angels and saints who are forever celebrating the worship of the living God.

In the Book of Revelation, St. John gives a magnificent description of this heavenly liturgy:

* * *

A throne was standing there in heaven, and on the throne was seated One whose appearance had a gemlike sparkle as of jasper and carnelian. . . . Surrounding this throne were twenty-four other thrones upon which were seated twenty-four elders; they were clothed in white garments and had crowns of gold on their heads. . . . The floor around the throne was like a sea of glass that was crystal-clear.

At the very center, around the throne itself, stood four living creatures covered with eyes front and back. . . . Day and night, without pause, they sing:

    "Holy, holy, holy, is the Lord God Almighty,

      He who was, and who is, and who is to come!"

Whenever these creatures give glory and honor and praise to the One seated on the throne, who lives forever and ever, the twenty-four elders fall

*down before the One seated on the throne, and worship him who lives
forever and ever. They throw down their crowns before the throne and
sing:*

    "O Lord our God, you are worthy
      to receive glory and honor and power!
    For you have created all things;
      by your will they came to be and were made!"

(Rv 4:2-11)

* * *

But in the midst of this eternal praise, a "new hymn" rises up. It
celebrates the incarnation, death, and victory of the Son of God, who
came to reveal to men the infinite love of his Father:

* * *

*As my vision continued, I heard the voices of many angels who
surrounded the throne and the living creatures and the elders. They were
countless in number, thousands and tens of thousands, and they all cried
out:*

    "Worthy is the Lamb that was slain
      to receive power and riches, wisdom and strength,
      honor and glory and praise!"

*Then I heard the voices of every creature in heaven and on earth and
under the earth and in the sea; everything in the universe cried aloud:*

    "To the One seated on the throne, and to the Lamb,
      be praise and honor, glory and might,
      forever and ever!"

*The four living creatures answered, "Amen," and the elders fell down
and worshiped.*

(Rv 5:11-14)

* * *

And so Christ is at the center of this liturgy. How could the Church
fail to be present, too? Where does the faithful Spouse remain, if not

close to the Bridegroom? This applies not only to the Church triumphant, but to the pilgrim, laboring, fighting Church, the Church of this earth. Indeed, every Preface of the Mass reminds us of it:

* * *

Through him the choirs of angels and all the powers of heaven praise and worship your glory. May our voices blend with theirs as we join in their unending hymn: Holy, holy, holy Lord, God of power and might, heaven and earth are full of your glory!

* * *

Be sure you understand this: the *Sanctus* of the Mass is infinitely more than a distant echo of the heavenly feast. It means that the Christian people is joining the jubilant assembly; that the earthly liturgy is incorporated into the liturgy of the angels; that we sinners have the right to take part in the heavenly worship in honor of the holiness of God and of the glory of Christ the Victor.

Do not imagine that I have strayed from our subject. I am aware that I am talking to you about mental prayer, and not about liturgical prayer. But the point is that mental prayer is also in very close contact with the world of the angels. An incident in the Bible makes this point very well. When night fell, Jacob fell asleep after placing a stone under his head. Actually, his was a mysterious sleep like that of Adam at the time of woman's creation, or like that of Abraham at the time of the Covenant. It was a prayer-sleep: *"I was sleeping, but my heart kept vigil"* (Sg 5:2).

During this sleep, Jacob saw a ladder, firmly planted on the earth, that reached up to the heavens. On this ladder, angels came and went, ascended and descended. Similarly when the Christian prays, the angels are immediately alerted and irresistibly drawn toward him. They come to convoke him to their great liturgy, and they fraternally draw him into it. There is nothing surprising about this. Does not Christ himself pray in the man or woman who is engaged in mental prayer? And Jesus declared, *"I solemnly assure you, you shall see the sky opened and the angels of God ascending and descending on the Son of Man"* (Jn 1:51).

62. The presence of Mary

I f we want to understand Mary's place in our life of prayer, we must begin by reflecting on her own prayer. It would be presumptuous to infringe on the communion of love between our infinitely perfect God and the most pure Virgin Mary. It is an inviolable holy of holies. At best, we can stand on the threshold, adore, and remain silent. But it is permissible, without violating the mystery, to seek to glimpse a few aspects of the prayer of the holiest of all God's creatures.

Above all, we are not to think of Mary's prayer as a reality remote from us in time and space. There is nothing more relevant within our grasp. Let us slip into her prayer, the way one slips into the shadows of a chapel.

In the presence of the Most High Majesty, she, the lowly daughter of man, adores. She sings a pure hymn of praise to the One who deigned to bend down over her lowliness, to do great things in her and through her.

Mary prays for, or rather in the name of, her innumerable children—an excellent way of praying for those we love. How many of these children forget their God! They fail to thank him for his lavish gifts, and do not beg his forgiveness or acknowledge his sovereignty! But fortunately, their Mother is there. What they neglect to do, she does in their place.

She intervenes for each one of us individually before her Son, offering the stammering prayer of one, the groping good intentions of another. She intercedes for all: for those who are suffering, for those threatened by temptation, for those who refuse to give themselves to God, and for those who are facing death.

Mary prays the way mothers do. I mean that she carries her children to her God, and offers them the way she once offered the Infant she held in her arms.

Do you see how I am answering your question on Mary's place in the prayer of Catholics? I will first speak to you of the place we hold in Mary's prayer. The reason is that our best prayer is the one the Virgin Mary offers in our name and on our behalf.

The Christian who wants to pray begins by kneeling close to his praying Mother. After he has been drawn into her recollection, he enters the company of his God through mental prayer. Then it is Mary's turn to become present to his prayer. If there is anything on earth that touches her motherly heart, it is the sight of one of her children trying to speak to the Lord and listen to him. Just as we shield a fragile flame from the wind with both hands, so Mary, with her all-powerful prayer, protects the mental prayer of her child.

63. The presence of Mary (continued)

Today, it is not I but a little boy named Bruno who will talk to you about mental prayer. It is a joy for me to send you a copy of the letter his mother sent me.

***

"Dear Father, in the *Cahier* for the month of August you wrote, 'The Christian who wants to pray begins by kneeling close to Mary in prayer.' This text would probably not have made such a great impression on me, had my reading not coincided with a family episode that I want to tell you about.

"Our four children had just spent a long evening with their cousins at our old summer cottage. It was very late—ten-thirty— and they were all getting sleepy. As I put them to bed, I told them, 'Just for this evening, sit on your beds for your night prayers.' I sat down myself, at the foot of one of the beds.

"I began the night prayer, and as I slowly recited the Lord's Prayer, I became deeply recollected. In fact, I didn't notice at first that the youngest, Bruno, was touched by it and got up. He came and knelt on the bed, leaning against me. He unfolded my hands, and slipped his hands into mine saying, 'Jesus.' I continued the prayer, deeply moved, and he knelt there motionless. The older children explained to me later on: 'He kept looking at you real hard, and then all of a sudden he got up.'

"As it happened, I chanced to read your text ten minutes later. If I hadn't read it, I would simply have had a tender memory of this tiny tot's delighted discovery. But now that I have read it, my prayer in union with Mary has been greatly helped."

64. Atheism and mental prayer

[Portion of a letter addressed to Father Caffarel by another French priest.]

"Father, in the Catholic circles that I frequent, there has been much talk of atheism since the Fathers of the Second Vatican Council considered the matter. It is as if, all of a sudden, people are becoming aware of this new and terrifying phenomenon. A short sentence by Bishop de Hnilica of Czechoslovakia, who came out of the concentration camps, caused quite a shock: 'One-third of the world is under the domination of atheism, which does not deny that it wants to conquer the whole world.'

"The reactions I note around me are no less varied than those of the Fathers during the 136th General Congregation of Vatican II. Equally varied are the causes to which this agonizing phenomenon is attributed.

"However, I am surprised that there is almost never any mention of what, to my mind, is one of the principal causes of atheism, at least in our Western nations: silence about God. Catholics, both priests and lay persons, rarely speak about God. I am not alone in noticing this. There is a cruel saying that goes back more than twenty years: 'Religion has had nothing to do with God for a very long time.'

"In recent years, I have had the opportunity to study the results of questionnaires sent to the faithful, asking their reactions to the Sunday sermons. I came to the same conclusion. A novelist—I don't know whether or not he is a practicing Christian—has noted this bankruptcy. Here is a passage from one of his novels:

* * *

"The truth is, that nobody talks about God any more. Nobody at all—and first of all the clergy. . . . In an age when material things reign supreme as never before, don't we need prophets? People who speak in season and out of season about God, the Creator and Master of the world as well as of all of life?" (R. Bésus)

* * *

"How can Christians hope that the upsurge of atheism will be halted, and the reign of God established on earth, if they do not first make God known to the world?"

* * *

My dear Father, have no fear. Your letter did not scandalize me. I have often made identical observations. Need I tell you that in retreats for priests—and I've made quite a few—I have not often heard anyone speak at length and in depth about God, his innermost life, and his perfections?

But why do we talk so rarely about God? That is the important question. To my mind, there is no doubt as to the answer. People don't talk about God, because they don't know him. We don't know him in the sense that the Scriptures give to the word "know." For the man of the Bible, to "know" means to have the concrete experience of a being. To know someone is to enter into personal relations with him. The Psalmist sang: *"Taste and see how good the Lord is"* (Ps 34:9). He knew God. Later on, St. John wrote: *"Eternal life* [begun on earth] *is this: to know you, the only true God"* (Jn 17:3). We know that for St. John, such knowledge is "communion."

Only those who know God experientially speak well of him (whether it be the pastor talking to his flock, the mother talking to her children, or the professor of theology talking to his class). The words of those who know God in this way, touch the innermost "self" of those they are addressing. This is the "heart" in the Biblical sense, the "center of the soul," as the mystics like to say. Their words have the power of awakening, stimulating and developing the sense of God in their audience.

But now a second question arises. Why are there so few of these "knowers of God," who can speak eloquently about him, and are impatient to make him known? I have no hesitation in answering: because the form of prayer is neglected, which the great doctors and spiritual writers have for centuries called "contemplation."

Objections are made to the use of this word. I admit it can be the source of ambiguity. In fact, God is not contemplated the way one contemplates a painting. Nothing comes between the contemplative and the God he contemplates. He finds this God within himself. He experiences, in the innermost depths of his soul, God's presence and love and light. But never mind the word. The fact is undeniable in its harsh reality: prayer is neglected and contemplation is discredited. Those who opt for a life of prayer are accused of deserting the cause of mankind, of ignoring the great and urgent apostolic tasks. So also are those who devote even a limited time to prayer. This is why some Trappists in recent years have felt twinges of conscience, and asked themselves whether they should not go to work in factories.

How far we have come from the conviction of the great Christian doctors—Augustine, the Gregories, Thomas Aquinas—who courageously affirmed the primacy of contemplation. They championed contemplation as a state of life, but also and first of all as a penetrating and delightful knowledge of God. Over and over again, they wrote commentaries on Christ's words to Martha: *"Martha, Martha, you are anxious and upset about many things; one thing only is required. Mary has chosen the better portion and she shall not be deprived of it"* (Lk 10:41-42).

St. Augustine commented on these words in a short but famous sentence: *"Martha turbabatur, Maria epulabatur."* It's not easy to give its richness of meaning in translation: "Martha busied herself, Mary enjoyed."

One would have to be completely ignorant of the history of the Church to dare claim that the contemplatives are ineffective persons. The detractors of the contemplative life would quickly change their minds if they read, attentively and in good faith, the lives of such saints as Bernard of Clairvaux, Catherine of Siena, Marie of the Incarnation, and so many others. Contemplation has always been the wellspring from which the boldest and most vigorous apostles of the Church renewed their missionary zeal.

God alone knows what his kingdom owes to so many hidden and unknown contemplatives. They don't all live in cloisters—many lay men and women are more truly contemplative than many monks.

My conviction stands firm. When contemplative life declines in the Church, error in diverse forms develops. The outstanding example is the militant atheism of our epoch, which one of the Fathers of Vatican Council II described as "the most serious error, the mortal illness of our time."

This tidal wave, which threatens to submerge the whole earth, will be repulsed only if the Church first makes an immense effort to nurture the contemplative life again in every milieu. Then there will be no more lamenting over the lack of apostles, and the prophets of the living God will multiply.

65. Black Mimoûna

S o your "young lions" spend their time quarreling! And you, their mother, grieve over it, and tell me things are getting worse all the time. (I must say, however, that I found your four boys very likable!)

Is it a matter of educational method? I am less sure of this than you. Far be it from me to counsel you against studying books concerned with education. I do fear, though, that you may lose a great deal of time pursuing miracle-pedagogy.

You remind me of the physician who unsuccessfully tries one cure after another, because he has misdiagnosed his patient's condition. Before searching for means of improving the situation, shouldn't you ask yourself what its true causes are?

Will you allow me to advance the hypothesis that at least one of these causes lies within yourself? A story taken from the golden legends of the Moslem saints will explain this to you more clearly than some long dissertation:

* * *

Abdalwâhid Ibn Zeid wanted to know who would be his neighbor in heaven, and the following answer was given him: "O Abdalwâhid, your neighbor will be Black Mimoûna." "And where is this Black Mimoûna?" he asked, with more boldness than discretion. "She is with the Banou So-and-So family, at Koûfa."

So Abdalwâhid went to Koûfa, and began to search for Mimoûna. He was told that she was a crazy woman who tended sheep over by the cemetery. He found her at prayer. The flock was grazing untended, and this was all the more extraordinary, because there were wolves intermingled with the sheep. The wolves did not eat the sheep, and the sheep were not afraid of the wolves. He was puzzled and asked, "How is it that these wolves get along so well with these sheep?"

Mimoûna answered, "I have improved my relations with my

Lord, and my Lord has improved the relations between the sheep and the wolves."

* * *

Every mother should ask herself, when she has trouble with her children, whether the real reason for it is that she is neglecting her relationship with God.

What is true at the level of the family is equally true at the level of society. Purely human means (such as a knowledge of psychology, teaching ability, authority and prestige) are powerless to bring about unity among men, in whom a virus of disunion has been imbedded since original sin. Above all, they are powerless to bring about the unity in charity which Christ demands so insistently.

The unity of the children of God is a work that only Christ can accomplish, and which he effectuates by sending the Holy Spirit. It was only after Pentecost that the disciples were said to be *"of one heart and one mind"* (Ac 4:32).

No one can be a worthy builder of unity unless he opens himself freely to the Spirit of God. How? By receiving the sacraments, but also through mental prayer. Without this prayer, the Holy Spirit who is given to us in the sacraments comes up against closed doors. Thanks to mental prayer, the Spirit's ascendancy becomes stronger and deeper with each passing day, and unity gradually becomes a reality. This unity is realized within us (for it is first of all within us that the uproar and division reign), but it is realized around us as well.

Then apostolic action proves its efficacy, not only in encouraging our brothers and sisters individually to serve the Lord, but also in achieving the unity of the children of God. It is this unity that Christ revealed as his deepest wish, during his great farewell prayer among his friends.

Make room for mental prayer in your life, and, I am sure, you will be able to write to me: "I have improved my relations with my Lord, and my Lord has improved the relations among my 'young lions,' whom I hope soon to call my 'young lambs'!"

66. In the breach

During the heat of the day, as the patriarch sat at the entrance of his tent, he looked up and saw three men, in reality Yahweh and two angels. He stood up, bowed low, and offered them hospitality. Then Yahweh renewed his promise to give him descendants, and disclosed to him that he was on his way to Sodom and Gomorrah to judge them.

Abraham then became the advocate of the criminal cities before God. His prayer, the first that we read in the Bible (cf. Gn 18:23-32), is a trusting, skillful, bold and pathetic intercession on behalf of the guilty. Abraham thus inaugurated the long line of intercessors who were to succeed one another in Israel from age to age.

About six centuries later, we might call Moses the prototype-intercessor. Weary of his people's unbelief, Yahweh declares to Moses: *"Let me alone, then, that my wrath may blaze up against them to consume them. Then I will make of you a great nation"* (Ex 32:10). From the first words, we understand that Moses is the one who *does not let God alone* to do as he pleases. Nor does Moses agree to break off relations with his people, even to receive a more glorious regency. He is the leader of these people by God's will, and so he will be their defender, their intercessor before the Lord himself.

Judges, kings and prophets, in the footsteps of Abraham and Moses, pleaded in their turn for this "stiff-necked" people and obtained mercy for them many times. But woe to the centuries when God found no intercessor: *"I have searched among them for someone who could build a wall or stand in the breach before me to keep me from destroying the land; but I found no one"* (Ezk 22:30).

Admire this portrait of the intercessor. He is the man who builds a rampart to protect his brothers, and keeps watch in the breach through which punishment might come.

Actually, all these intercessors of our Bible are but figures, rough drafts of the great and only Intercessor: Jesus Christ. Here is the man whom God is seeking. Standing in the breach, both arms outstretched, he intervenes. More effectively than Abraham, he pleads for the criminal world. And because he has united himself to human nature in the Incarnation—*et Verbum caro factum est*—human nature has been reconciled with the Father for all time.

Once and for all, Jesus Christ offered himself, and rebuilt the bridge between mankind and God. In a sense, his mission as an intercessor is completed. But it is equally true that he wants to continue his function of intercession on earth until the end of time. In order to accomplish this, he depends on us, his disciples. It is now our turn to remain in the breach, and keep watch. It is our turn to plead for the vast multitude of men and women everywhere, but first and in a special way for the people among whom it is our predestined mission to incarnate Christ and carry on his intercession.

Several times in my priestly life, I thought I discerned the Lord's strategy. In order not to turn away from a certain sinful family, from a certain dechristianized village, he raises up within them a prayerful person. And he blesses the place, the human group, where he has a beloved child. It may be a crippled young man, a humble peasant girl, or a poor country pastor afire with prayer.

The prayer of these intercessors is none other than Christ's own prayer. Otherwise it would be nothing. It is the prayer of Christ kindled within them by the Spirit of Christ, one of whose proper names is Paraclete: advocate, defender, intercessor. Undoubtedly, while the Holy Spirit pleads for those in whom he dwells, he also intercedes for all mankind in them and through them.

The glorious Christ, at the right hand of the Father, translates in heaven everything that all intercessors, inspired by the Spirit, ask in their deficient human language on earth. For the risen Lord lives and *never ceases interceding for us* (cf. 1 Jn 2:1; Heb 7:25).

Intercession is truly one of the great words in the vocabulary of prayer. It is a truly sublime function. It witnesses at once to a great love of God, and to a great love of men.

67. With outstretched arms

I have just reread, in *Le Visage de mon frère* (My Brother's Face) by D.G. Mukerji, a page that brings out the great power of prayer. Here is a summary of its essential points.

* * *

Toward the end of his life, a holy man withdrew into a mountain cave in order to be better able to find God. The peasants of the vicinity never failed to have fruit and biscuits brought to him, and sometimes they would go up the mountain to him themselves. The youths protested against these prodigal gifts for a useless man. But the old men silenced the young rationalists: "We must send offerings to a holy man, whether or not he lives for the good of anyone. Isn't holiness the great jewel of existence?"

After twenty years, one day the holy man was found dead, lying at the entrance of the cave. Six weeks later, a terrible crime was committed in the village. Everyone was filled with disgust and fear. The elders went off to fast and pray. Suddenly one of them cried out, "I've discovered the secret." Standing before the assembled peasants, he explained what he meant: "It's true that the holy man never lifted a finger to help us the whole time he lived in his cave, or brought succor to the destitute, or cared for even one sick person. But virtue begot virtue, life brought forth a better life. All was well with us. Not a single man took his brother's life as long as the saint lived. Isn't it all very clear? He never worked for us, but his lion's presence kept the wolf of misfortune away from our doors."

* * *

This story reminds us irresistibly of a great page of the Bible in Chapter XVII of Exodus:

* * *

At Rephidim, Amalek came and waged war against Israel. Moses, therefore, said to Joshua, "Pick out certain men, and tomorrow go out and engage Amalek in battle. I will be standing on top of the hill with the staff of God in my hand." So Joshua did as Moses told him: he engaged Amalek in battle after Moses had climbed to the top of the hill with Aaron and Hur. As long as Moses kept his hands raised up, Israel had the better of the fight, but when he let his hands rest, Amalek had the better of the fight. Moses' hands, however, grew tired; so they put a rock in place for him to sit on. Meanwhile Aaron and Hur supported his hands, one on one side and one on the other, so that his hands remained steady till sunset. And Joshua mowed down Amalek and his people with the edge of the sword (Ex 17:8-13).

* * *

Amalek's soldiers could not understand what power was resisting their impetuous attacks. The Israelite army, badly trained and much smaller than theirs, could not account for the resistance. It never occurred to them that the man scarcely visible at the top of the hill, more poorly armed than his own troops, was the cause of their defeat. God was present in him, because he was praying. And the divine omnipotence that emanated from him strengthened his men for combat and protected them like an invisible and inviolable rampart.

We can fully understand the two stories I have just recounted, only in the light of the Gospel. On another hill a man also stretched out his arms. Two nails held them up. And from him, God's Power was poured out upon the world. There is nothing in space or time that escapes this Power, the Holy Spirit. It sustains in their combats all who welcome it and surrender to it. In them this Power works mightily, and through them it overwhelms the demons and their cohorts.

Moses' prayer and the prayer of the holy man of India were efficacious because the Power that manifested itself at Calvary came to them, without their knowing just what it was. The prayer of Christians is powerful because it is united to the inexhaustible wellspring of divine energy, the heart of the Crucified praying his great filial prayer.

68. To pray is to cooperate with God

As I read your letter, I thought: "Why not answer the questions of a Protestant by a Protestant?" I picked up a book in my library that I have reread many times, and which has always given me renewed inspiration to pray. I refer to *Le Problème de la prière* (The Problem of Prayer) by Fernand Ménégoz. Certainly, I do not agree with all of this author's theses. But what fervent conviction, what faith in the primordial importance of prayer! Here is the very importance that, you write, seems to escape you.

The core of his message stems from the purest Biblical tradition. It is condensed in one of the many definitions of prayer that can be gleaned from his book:

* * *

Christian prayer is the cry of a heart conquered by the grace of the sovereign God, whose supreme joy is to "cooperate" with God and to see the divine work of salvation triumph in human society.

* * *

There is a danger that we will accept this definition without measuring its full significance. The author, for his part, did not hesitate to deploy considerable erudition to justify it throughout the five hundred pages of his book. He first attacks an error that he considers to be the most formidable of all. This consists in speaking of Christian prayer solely from man's point of view. It is as if prayer were only one human activity among others, which man could perform left to his own resources. It is as if God were just another person, to whom we address our requests, and remain on good terms with, but who remains external to us.

Fernand Ménégoz forces us to reverse our perspective. In many different ways, he repeats that in order to understand prayer we have to start out not from man, but from God. We have to start from God at work in the world and in each of us, accomplishing the work of salvation. St. Paul presents this to us in a vigorous synthesis in the first chapter of the Epistle to the Ephesians: the gathering together in his risen Son of all those who open themselves to his grace through faith.

This God, who never ceases his work of forgiving, regenerating, and saving, invites the believer to work with him. And that's what prayer is: cooperating with God, so that in each one of us the work of God may be realized, his name be blessed, his kingdom come, and his will be done.

Such a prayer is fundamentally devoid of self-interest.

* * *

In place of the principle that tends to make the Godhead the servant of man, it substitutes the opposite principle that makes man the totally dependent servant of God. It yearns for the revelation of the glory of "the Lord of heaven and earth" and requests on man's behalf only what will make this glory shine forth.

* * *

But the Christian does not cooperate only in God's work within him during prayer. He also cooperates in the work of the sovereign and holy God in the whole world. This prayer is a combat more than a labor. However, the Christian is not alone in persevering in this labor and this combat. The Spirit of Christ quickens him, leads him, sustains him, and encourages him.

When Fernand Ménégoz considers the future of Christianity and the world, the scholar in him is filled with the vehemence of the prophets, and he gives us dire warnings. If theology persists in disregarding the importance of prayer, if Christians cling to an egocentric prayer commanded solely by their own interests, if, under the influence of hostile philosophies, they renounce prayer, then, he predicts, our century will end in spiritual darkness and scientific barbarism. *"Either Christianity will conquer the world through prayer, or it will perish." "This is a matter of life or death for Christianity."*

Conversely, once authentic Christian prayer, inspired only by the interests and the glory of God, is rediscovered, then Christianity will experience a new purity and a new expansion. Thanks to Christianity, mankind will rise to a higher civilization.

* * *

Christianity conquers . . . only in communities where the eruptive and "primitive" spirit of evangelical prayer continues to unfurl its action.

Prayer is the missionary phenomenon par excellence.

The only truly "civilizing" power is the praying Church.

The "Ecclesia orans" (praying Church) is the one and only wellspring of a real, profound and enduring progress, of a regenerating progress both for the individual and for society.

* * *

And why does prayer have such great power? Because to repeat once more, it is not man's activity but God's action within man, in which man participates. Christ said, *"My Father is at work until now, and I am at work as well"* (Jn 5:17). The man and woman who pray contact God's all-powerful action within themselves, surrender to it, cooperate with it, and offer it the means of penetrating a world that would otherwise remain closed to its riches.

"Blessed are they who hunger and thirst" (Mt 5:6)

The road that leads to perfect union with God is a long one. Prayer alternates between desire and supplication, combat and fidelity. Little by little it is purified in patience and selflessness, until it becomes in its totality a pure desire for the glory of God.

The appetite for happiness, so deeply rooted in man's heart, is one of the most powerful stimulants of our spiritual progress. Even so, far from fearing this appetite, we must allow it to be strengthened in mental prayer.

69 *Happiness*—Hunger for the absolute, akin to the appetite for happiness, combines with it to draw us toward God. It already witnesses to the work of the Holy Spirit within us.

70 *This hunger for the absolute*—But on earth, our need for happiness and for the absolute cannot be fully satisfied. That is why our prayer is basically the supplication of exiles.

71 *The groanings of the Spirit*—This is a supplication vibrant with hope. Obviously, we cannot hope to see God here and now, but he invites us without further delay to an ever-growing intimacy with him.

72 *"Hope will not leave us disappointed"* (Rm 5:5)—In any event, our desire for God must be purified in patience. There is still too much "covetousness" in it.

73 *Prayer must be a fast before it becomes a feast*—Let us be on our guard against clinging more to the Lord's gifts than to the Lord himself.

74 *The giver or the gifts?*—God permits "spiritual dryness" and "nights" precisely so that our hope may be stripped of any alloys.

75 *Is it for nothing?*—This purification of the desire for God is in no sense its attenuation. The purer this desire, the more it becomes an

insatiable thirst for the living God, a thirst which is vehemently expressed in the Psalms and in the writings of the great mystics.

76   *"Like parched land"* (Ps 143:6)—Our desire for union with God will be granted some day. This union will be the work of agapé love, for its origin lies not in man's heart, but in the heart of God.

77   *Begging from God*—This is the sign by which we can recognize the presence and the progress of the love of charity in us: when the desire for the Lord's glory becomes the one and only motivating force of our whole spiritual life.

78   *The glory of God comes first.*

69. Happiness

Y our attitude toward happiness reminds me of the response of an audience of students before whom I developed the following theme: the great benefit of mental prayer is that it awakens our appetite for happiness if it is dormant, and intensifies it if it is already alive and well. During the discussion and exchange of views that followed, their reactions surprised me.

One of the students asked, "Should we not rather expect mental prayer to satisfy this need in us?" Another student suggested that the goal of all spiritual seekers is to arrive at holy indifference, and that both Buddhists and Christians aspire to this as the supreme wisdom. For isn't it only when we bring our appetite for happiness under control, that we finally achieve the inner calm required for spiritual progress?

The debate was lively and prolonged. The students were on the defensive, as if I were threatening a hard-earned tranquility of theirs, that consisted precisely in the suppression of their hunger for happiness. However, I think I succeeded in convincing them that this very yearning could be the best stimulus to their spiritual progress. Shall I succeed in convincing you as well?

Those who lose their desire for happiness soon die of inanition. Conversely, those who fearlessly nurture this desire derive their greatest joys from it—and their bitterest disappointments as well. In any event, they are intensely alive. They do, of course, run the risk of despairing of creatures. But isn't this risk the greatest opportunity, or rather the greatest grace, if it makes them understand that their appetite for happiness can be sated by nothing less than God himself?

The fact remains that prayer can act as a kind of filter for this appetite, and thus prevent it from being corrupted. The great men and women of prayer begin early to have an intense craving for happiness. And they want nothing less than absolute happiness. That is why God detaches them from everything. Incidentally, detachment is not indifference. Rather, it enables them to reach out to all creatures in their secret hunger for happiness. It impels them to draw others to the God whom they themselves are seeking in hope with their whole being.

They do not only look to God to fill their human capacity for happiness. He, for his part, hollows out within them totally new capacities. This enlarging of their spiritual potential causes them suffering, but it also increases their hope. They realize that God excavates only in order to give more lavishly.

I cannot advise you too insistently, as you begin your mental prayer, to concentrate on your fundamental desire for happiness, rather than on the various appetites on the periphery of your being. Free this desire from everything that obstructs or overlays it. Direct it toward the One for whom it yearns perhaps without realizing it. It will soon come alive, and become a permanent guest within you, perhaps a very disturbing one. You will no longer be able to satisfy it with mere reflections of happiness. It will constantly importune you to attain to a greater knowledge and possession of the God who gives joy.

70. This hunger for the absolute

Yesterday as I listened to you, I felt as if somewhere I had already heard what you were telling me. But try as I might to ransack the archives of my memory, I found nothing. Today the memory you awakened in me is emerging from the shadows, and in such detail that I am surprised. Perhaps it will offer you some light.

A young priest-friend of mine found it increasingly difficult to concentrate, and this made it impossible for him to pursue his studies. He consulted a psychiatrist, and afterwards told me the advice he had received. Actually, the psychiatrist's various recommendations could be summed up in one counsel: *Age quod agis.* (Do what you are doing). The psychiatrist explained, "Put your mind on what you are doing. Perform conscious acts, and begin by simply recording the sensations that are offered to you. You wash your hands: experience the freshness of the water. You eat a peach: experience its delicious taste. Your trouble is that you are divided. Your consciousness, engrossed by other things, is only half-aware of what you are doing."

I remember objecting strongly, for I had the feeling that the advice my friend had received could lead him completely astray. So I said to him, "I challenge you to succeed in putting your mind totally on sensations!" I questioned him to verify whether my reaction was well-founded. "You admit you cannot concentrate, but that is probably not the only symptom of what is going on within you. When you drive a car, don't you always go a little faster than you should? As if you were in a hurry to reach your destination, and were going to find there something you have long been pursuing? And isn't it true that you don't know how to relax? That you are always disappointed in things and in people, and first of all in yourself?" He agreed.

"Well then," I added, "here is my diagnosis. You are inhabited by a hunger for the absolute which, since it is never satisfied, makes it impossible for you to stop seeking. This is nothing else than the need for God, which has grown in you through your industrious and fervent years in the seminary. And today you are, to use the words of the Psalmist, *'like the hind that longs for the running waters'* (Ps 42:2). You are like *'parched land'* (Ps 143:6).

"The difficulty you experience in concentrating, and the symptoms to which I have just drawn your attention, and which you acknowledge, are simply manifestations of a profound need of which you have not been aware until now. It is not by begging for meager contentments from creatures that you will be cured, but by understanding that your hunger can be satisfied only by God."

The next morning, I was expecting my friend for breakfast as usual. When he did not come, I decided to breakfast alone. An hour and a half later, he came into my office and explained why he was late. "After my Mass, as I was beginning my thanksgiving, I became aware of the presence within me of a hunger for the absolute that I had never yet identified. And so I directed this hunger toward God. It was as if I were emancipating a prayer that had long been held captive. Time passed without my being aware of it. Although I am usually tormented by distractions and—I am not proud to admit it—in a hurry to finish, today I spent two hours in mental prayer."

To make me understand what had happened to him, my friend

used an amusing image. "During these two hours when a great peace had settled in my soul, I had only to place my adorations, petitions, praises, intentions on an escalator that carried them straight up to God."

Am I mistaken in thinking that there is in you, as in my friend, an as yet unidentified need for the absolute, that communicates impatience and anxiety to your whole life? Learn to recognize this need, stop focusing it on creatures that can only disappoint and exasperate it, and turn it deliberately toward God, its one real object. I don't know if you will have the same experience as my friend, who was prepared for it by a very generous life. At any rate, I am sure that you will get rid of this indefinable anxiety that harasses you, this ever-renewed sense of disappointment.

Hunger for the absolute is not just one aspiration among many others. It is the fundamental aspiration of every human person. It may be denied or repressed, but it cannot be eliminated. It is part and parcel of us, the substance of our spiritual being. On earth, in heaven, in hell, nobody can rid himself of it the way one throws off a coat. In hell it is, as it were, in the pure state. The damned are condemned to their need for the absolute, but are permanently deprived of their object. Theirs is a ravenous hunger that has nothing to devour, an inextinguishable fire that has nothing to consume except the one in whom it burns.

In heaven, this aspiration is fulfilled at the very instant that one attains the beatific vision of the living God. *"I shall be content in your presence"* (Ps 17:15).

During our sojourn on earth, mental prayer is the privileged hour to liberate this hunger from the desires that parasitize it, and from the diversions that distract us from it, by enabling it to rediscover its object: God. It goes without saying that this hunger will never be fully appeased here below. In a sense, mental prayer even intensifies it. But once it has been identified, it is no longer a cause for anxiety. Those in whom it lives and develops, remember with joy the saying that Pascal placed on Christ's lips: "Be consoled. You would not be seeking me, if you had not already found me."

71. The groanings of the Spirit

M y dear Steve, I would like to talk about a sentence in your letter: "It disturbs me to hear it said, over and over, that the Holy Spirit prays within us with *'ineffable groanings.'* To me, this expression seems terribly sad!" Am I wrong to suspect that you refrained from adding: "I can't stand people who groan"? Aren't you telling me that in your view, the Holy Spirit should instead inspire us to shout triumphant hosannas?

Do you know the author of the expression that you are incriminating? None other than St. Paul! Now, you'll certainly agree that he was a virile, militant soul, straining toward victory. If he used these words that displease you, it must surely have been because he could think of none better to translate the prayer of the Holy Spirit that he discovered deep within himself. Yes, a continual groaning rose from his strong and impassioned soul.

Let's go back to the context, to the eighth chapter of the Epistle to the Romans. It will then be clear to you that this word "groaning" was certainly not chosen at random. It recurs three times in three consecutive paragraphs. It is closely related to "await" (which appears three times) and "hope" (five times).

What, then, is *awaited, hoped for* with *groanings?* Our liberation. Although we aspire with all our being to be united to the Father, who calls us and offers us eternal life in his love and happiness, we are held captive by the earth, by time, and by our bodies. And when our love for our Father grows strong, the hope within us becomes vehement, and our groanings more poignant.

According to St. Paul, it is not only the Christian soul that is haunted by these groanings. It is also nature, the entire created universe: the stars and the earth, the desert and the forest, the crops and the animals. A muffled, continuous groaning, like a vast, unending ocean swell, rises toward God from this world which aspires, without knowing it, to *"share in the glorious freedom of the children of God"* (Rm 8:21).

The Christian knows things that are hidden from the rest of Creation. The groanings of all men (who are often as ignorant as inanimate things of what they hope for) are united, in the Christian's heart, with the groanings of the natural universe. That is, in the heart of a child impatient for reunion with his Father.

We are far removed from groanings that might be the sentimental plaint of a weak soul. It is really a metaphysical surge, a cosmic aspiration rising from the innermost depths of creation. However, this surge would remain fruitless if the Spirit did not join his *"ineffable groanings"* to the groanings of creatures, to turn them into a prayer to which God cannot turn a deaf ear.

These universal groanings are, to use St. Paul's forceful image, the groans of a Creation in the pangs of a mysterious and awesome childbirth: the bringing forth of the Kingdom of God.

72. *"And this hope will not leave us disappointed"* (Rm 5:5)

The hour of despair is really the hour of hope! You are going through the harsh experience of discovering spiritual weakness, your incapacity to serve God. Your failures overwhelm you, and your stagnation discourages you. All these things indicate to me that God is at work in your life. First of all, Christ captivated and conquered you, and you responded with enthusiasm. Now he has set out to train you. He has begun by making you discover your radical poverty. You will probably have to go still further in this discovery, and consent fully to your wretchedness, accepting it "in truth."

When you no longer revolt against this misery of yours but, like St. Paul, *"boast"* about it (cf. 2 Cor 12:5), the work of grace within you can make rapid progress. What do the weaknesses of man matter, since the grace of God suffices (cf. 2 Cor 12:9)?

As you can see, this presupposes a turnabout in your perspective, a conversion of your underlying attitude. You had set out to conquer your salvation, whereas you have to *hope* for it. Call to mind another experience, already far in the past. You had just met Nadine, and there was no doubt in your mind that she was going to be your wife. But she did not share your conviction.

I remember your impatience and tenseness. You were a young man accustomed to success, and you were fuming. There are victories that one cannot win by force of arms, but you didn't know that then. So many young people imagine that with power, intelligence, or money, one can acquire everything! You had to discover the world of free giving, which is also the world of love. You had to approach this young woman not like a conqueror, but with "sighs." This word sounds ridiculous, but it is very expressive.

The same is true of God's gifts. He withholds them from anyone who expects to earn them. On the other hand, he grants them to the one who "sighs" after them. I mean to the one who "hopes," who expects them solely from God's generosity.

So, contrary to your belief, your poverty is your great claim to the Lord's benefactions. Poverty germinates hope, and hope cannot be disappointed. It's the rich man who is sent away empty-handed, precisely because he is already satisfied and has nothing to hope for. The one who is starving, for his part, is given his fill. Reread the Beatitudes. Who are declared blessed? The poor. And why? Because, deprived of earthly goods, they are ready and willing to receive God's gifts.

It is true that poverty alone would not suffice to beget hope, if it did not rely on the Lord's promises. But these promises have been given to mankind since the day of the first sin (cf. Gn 3:15). As a result, mankind has never completely sunk into despair.

Open your Bible and follow the trail of hope. Look at Abraham, suffering from the most cruel poverty of not having any children. God promises him a posterity as innumerable as the stars on a summer night. But his hope must be pure, and rooted in God's power alone. Whence interminable delays. Abraham is called the father of believers. He could just as well be called the father of those who hope.

In the cases of the Israelites in Egypt and of the Jews deported to Babylon, God intervenes when all human hope has failed, and they finally turn to him. It's always the same pedagogy. God can grant his gifts only to those who hope. In order to arouse hope in a man, there is often no better way than to plunge him into poverty. Then, between despair and hope in God, perhaps man will choose the latter.

Another point worth noting is that Abraham hopes for a merely human posterity, and the Jews hope only for a national liberator. But God wants to give them more. To Abraham he chooses to give a spiritual posterity, and to the Jews he offers liberation from a slavery far worse than that to the Romans, the slavery of sin. God will do the same with you. He inspires you to hope that he will give you his strength, to enable you to practice virtue. He will give you far more: his love and his close friendship. He will give himself to you. What matters to God is that man, in discovering his poverty, opens himself to hope. Then he fulfills this hope, far beyond human expectations.

So open yourself to hope!

But you must realize that hope is not passivity. It expresses itself through effort. It was hope that made Abraham give up his country, his home and his comfort. It was hope that set him in motion. It was hope that sustained the Israelites during their forty-year odyssey in the wilderness. It was hope again that inspired the columns of poor Jews, filled with song and joy, as they returned to their ruined Jerusalem. The person who hopes disengages himself. As long as he hopes, he refuses to settle down. The person who hopes goes forward. As long as he hopes, he continues to advance, because his treasure lies ahead. I invite you to set out boldly on the road of hope, without looking back.

Over the years, your hope will change. At the start, it will probably be a matter of the will—of a will founded on faith in God's promises. But as yours is a living hope, it will grow with your increasing awareness of your poverty and your love for God. Indeed, love and hope are inseparable. Can the love that has discovered a treasure, fail to aspire to its full possession? The same is true of the person who has encountered the Lord. Little by little, hope takes hold of his entire being. His intellect aspires to an ever more perfect knowledge of God. His heart is impatient to share total intimacy with him. His innermost being cries out its need to possess him, and to be possessed by him.

I am not inventing this. You have only to read the works of the great spiritual men and women. At one stage of their development, their hope always becomes an unquenchable thirst for the living God. And their hope is not mocked. Jesus Christ offers them the living water of which he said: *"Whoever drinks the water I give him will never be thirsty; no, the water I give shall become a fountain within him, leaping up to provide eternal life"* (Jn 4:14).

As your hope intensifies, it will be purified, just like the love from which it emanates. The *hope for oneself* of the early stages (one needs help of one kind or another, or perhaps one aspires to the sensible presence of God) gradually becomes *hope for what God wants*. One no longer hopes for oneself, but for God. It is for his sake, that we want to be united to him. It is for his glory, and not first of all for our own joy.

The experience of certain mystics follows along the lines of this purification. Their hope ceases to be a burning, panting, restless hunger, and becomes a peaceable surrender into the hands of God. They have discovered that God is seeking them far more than they are seeking him. Take, for instance, the Moslem who wrote: "A voice cried out to me: 'O Aboû Yazîd, what do you desire?' I answered: 'I desire not to desire, because I am the desired one and You are the One who desires!' "

I have been speaking to you of the Christian who lives by hope, as if he were an isolated being. In reality, he is immersed in the vast created universe, and he knows it. He wants to be at one with all creatures. He hears the muffled groans of those who, St. Paul tells us, aspire to share in the glorious liberty of the children of God. The Christian lends them his heart and his voice so that, within him, their groaning may become hope.

The Christian senses his union especially with his brothers and sisters. He feels that he is united to all the poor of the earth in their search for bread, for a roof over their heads, for a homeland, for a little love and respect, and (often without knowing it) for a God. He feels that he is united to all the rich, too, whose power, wealth, and pleasures bring them only disappointment. It is their nature, too, to aspire to an absolute happiness. In the midst of all who are deprived of authentic hope, the Christian is the brother in whom their desires, despairs, and disappointments are melded into a prayer of hope.

The Christian's strength, his fidelity in hope, stems from his belonging to the people of hope, to the Church. He is glad to know that he is in communion with the hope of all God's children. This hope is certainly an expectation of divine help, but first and above all it is a yearning for the Day of the Lord. On that day, Christ will return in glory to raise the dead, to create a new heaven and a new earth, and to offer himself to his Father's love, with the great multitude of those who have been saved. Then God will be "all and in all," and hope will be a thing of the past. The infinite happiness of God will have become the portion of all his creatures.

It seems as though I have said very little about mental prayer. But the truth is that mental prayer has been constantly present in my thoughts, as I was writing to you. For mental prayer is the privileged moment when hope is renewed, and finds expression. During mental prayer, hope attains new intensity as it remembers the Lord's promises. In the aridity of prayer, hope becomes more fervent. When the Lord allows himself to be glimpsed, hope hastens toward him in leaps and bounds.

"This hope will not leave us disappointed" (Rm 5:5)

73. *Prayer must be a fast before it becomes a feast*

Patience and impatience are two of the many virtues that mental prayer requires. I use the word "impatience" advisedly. Granted, it is not included in the official catalogue of the virtues. And yet isn't impatience the daughter of love? How could the lover bear separation from the beloved, and not burn with the impatient desire to rejoin, possess and be united with the beloved? But you certainly don't need any invitation to impatience. You are well acquainted with it. On the other hand, it seems that you are less accustomed to the practice of patience. I would like to discuss patience with you, because it is absolutely necessary for anyone who wants to attain great heights in the practice of mental prayer.

You've been in the seminary scarcely six months, and already you are disheartened not to have reached the summits of prayer! I beg of you, be patient, or—if you prefer—be patiently impatient. It is a good thing to eagerly desire union with God, but the road is long, and the path is steep. One must set out with a calm step, and the regular breathing of the man who wants to reach great heights.

Patience, patience, my dear Francis, and don't forget what the etymology of the word can teach us. It comes from the Latin *pati*: to suffer, to endure. If you are resolved to endure, to hold out, to confront the desert and the night, then be confident. But you must reaffirm your resolve often. It will be threatened many times, especially at the hour of mental prayer.

Certain spiritual authors of an earlier time, speaking of the trials of prayer, used a very strong expression. They said that we must *suffer God*. In other words, we must consent to the implacable, ingenious and persevering work of the Holy Spirit within us. Very gradually, he causes the "old man" to die, so that the "new man" can come forth freed from his dross, like glistening metal coming out of the furnace.

You must have a courageous patience, like that of Jacob wrestling with the angel through the long night. Although injured, he refused to let go. That is why, at dawn, he obtained the blessing of his terrifying adversary (cf. Gn 32:25-30).

A distant memory comes to mind as I write you: an old monk's invitation to patience addressed to a novice. It is in *Miguel Mañara*, the

"mystery" of the great Polish poet Milosz. Before bidding you adieu, I
shall copy a few lines from this book for your reflection:

* * *

"Love and haste do not get along well, Mañara. Love is
measured by patience. A smooth, even step: that is the air of love,
whether it is sauntering between two jasmine hedges with a young
girl on its arm, or walking alone between two rows of tombstones.
Patience . . .
"An over-passionate hunger is also a temptation. Weeds and
roots must be pulverized by bovine jaws in a beautiful meadow
during the long, long hours of summer. . . .
"For prayer must be a fast before it becomes a feast. It must be
nakedness of heart before becoming a heavenly cloak rustling
with the sounds of the world. A day may come when God will allow
you to enter abruptly like an axe into the flesh of the tree, to fall
dizzily like a stone into the darkness of the water, and to slip with a
song into the heart of metal, like fire."

74. The giver or the gifts?

Frances, thank the Lord who is helping you to pray. The desire for
mental prayer, the attention to God that comes so easily during
prayer, and the joyous fervor that wells up in you like a living spring,
are precious graces. You see, God himself often chooses to teach his
children how to pray. In order to make them decide to set out on the
path of mental prayer, he comes to their rescue in a manner perceptible
to the senses.
It is important to realize that after a while, he will withdraw his
graces of initiation. This is so that the soul, once weaned, will go
forward in pure faith. The day will come, and perhaps soon, when you
will be required to believe in dryness and darkness, what you are now
experiencing in fervor and light. Prepare yourself for this new phase.
As I read your letters, I sometimes fear that you are clinging more to the
gifts than to the Giver. What matters is to be pleasing to God, not to
delight in his graces. This is as true of the sensible graces received
during mental prayer, as it is of all God's gifts. If they are not used as

paths to intimacy with God, they will become enslaving idols.

This language is probably too abstract for a high school girl. An illustration taken from a movie may make my thought clearer to you.

* * *

A very poor young peasant couple are living in a cottage. On the wife's birthday, the husband goes to the neighboring town with his meager savings. It's crazy to spend this money—but when one is in love . . . He brings back a precious package, and quickly hands it to his wife. She is delighted to find a pair of stockings. This is something wonderful for her because, being a poor peasant woman, she has never worn any. She admires them, and can't stop turning them over and over, caressing them tenderly. She does not notice that her husband is sad, and turns away as if he were intruding. He comes back, and finds her still completely engrossed with the stockings. Finally, he can't stand it any more and shows his vexation. The young woman understands at once. She grabs some scissors, and cuts the stockings to pieces. She recoils from anything that can turn her eyes away from her beloved, even for an instant. And she rushes into her husband's arms.

* * *

Frances, may the Lord's gifts be an invitation to rush into his arms, and not a temptation to delight in them for their own sake.

75. Is it for nothing?

Are you familiar with the very strange story at the beginning of the Book of Job?

* * *

One day, when the sons of God came to present themselves before the Lord, Satan also came among them. And the Lord said to Satan, "Whence do you come?" Then Satan answered the Lord and said, "From roaming the earth and patrolling it." And the Lord said to Satan, "Have you noticed my servant Job, and that there is no one on earth like him, blameless

*and upright, fearing God and avoiding evil?" But Satan answered the
Lord and said, "Is it for nothing that Job is God-fearing? Have you not
surrounded him and his family and all that he has with your protection?
You have blessed the work of his hands, and his livestock are spread over
the land. But now put forth your hand and touch anything that he has, and
surely he will blaspheme you to your face"* (Jb 1:6-11).

* * *

"Is it *for nothing* that he loves you?" Satan sneers. Does he cherish
you, or does he cherish the gifts that he has received from your hands in
such abundance? It is a perfidious and gross insinuation. Is Job's love
for God nothing but a vile self-love, cleverly camouflaged? Job is put to
the test, and he proves that his love for God is indeed authentic.

A sentence in your last letter alerted me: "I can't fight off a certain
sadness at having lost this intimacy with Christ in my mental prayer. It
helped me so much these last few years amid the family difficulties, as
you know so well." As I read this, I wondered whether you are sufficiently vigilant in ferreting out whatever self-concern there may be in
your mental prayer. God forbid that I should discourage your desire for
intimacy with Christ. I am thoroughly convinced that it is a grace. But is
this desire sufficiently stripped of self-seeking? Is it "for nothing" that
you love Christ?

Since that wonderful retreat of 1949, God has often granted you a
keen sense of his presence and his love. This was to encourage you in
the life of mental prayer. Have you perhaps come to take it for granted?
Have you perhaps allowed yourself, without realizing it, to practice
mental prayer more for the delight of the Lord's presence, than simply
for his glory? At any rate, this is a question I invite you to ask yourself.
When God grants us sensible graces, it is very difficult to keep a subtle
self-love from mingling in with our love for him. It is hard to keep a
selfish desire to possess him from insinuating itself into our will to
glorify him.

That is why a purification is necessary. This probably explains the
"spiritual dryness" you are experiencing at this time. Place your trust in
the grace at work within you, but do not fail to cooperate with it.

This is what I would advise you to do. From the start of your mental
prayer, affirm to God that you have come to it because it is his will. In

order to please him, place yourself completely and unconditionally at his service. Accept in advance to receive no sensible grace, and even ask him not to grant you any, if that can contribute to the coming of his Kingdom. I know that we are instinctively reluctant to talk like this to the Lord. However, prayer of this sort has a miraculously purifying effect on the heart.

Prayerful souls would be purified much more quickly, if they surrendered themselves in this way into the hands of God. He is eager to prune his vine, so that it may bear more abundant and more succulent fruit. If these souls grow discouraged, or clamor like spoiled children for new sensible graces, how can they expect to make any spiritual progress?

Set out on this path courageously. I say "courageously" not as a manner of speaking, but because that is the right word to use. This phase of purification is a tough one. It takes great valor to persevere in it, to accept the apparent death of the feelings, the intellect, and the heart. But that's what it's all about. Our sensibility, by dint of being weaned from all gratification, seems to die. Our intellect, deprived of all life, paralyzed in its meditation, also seems to die. Our heart becomes insensible and, as it were, incapable of loving. We can understand why a spiritual writer of earlier times spoke of the "sacrifice of mental prayer."

Great faith is also needed if we are not to be led to think that this time of mental prayer is wasted. We must be convinced that this death prepares a resurrection, that *"unless the grain of wheat falls to the earth and dies, it remains just a grain of wheat. But if it dies, it produces much fruit"* (Jn 12:24).

Mental prayer, with the trials it holds for us, is really the crucible in which our love for God is purified, and attains sparkling radiance.

76. *"Like parched land"* (Ps 143:6)

M y dear Father, why do you ask me whether, during mental prayer, we can surrender without scruples to our desire for union with God? Isn't the answer to be found in our breviary? For the breviary makes us put on the desire for God which burned in the Psalmist's heart, and found expression in such poignant accents:

* * *

* * *

"My soul thirsts for you like parched land" (Ps 143:6).
"O God, you are my God whom I seek;
for you my flesh pines and my soul thirsts
like the earth, parched, lifeless and without
water.
Thus have I gazed toward you in the sanctuary
to see your power and your glory . . ." (Ps 63:2-3).
"As the hind longs for the running waters,
so my soul longs for you, O God.
Athirst is my soul for God, the living
God.
When shall I go and behold the face of
God?" (Ps 42:2-3).

* * *

Theology also answers your question. It is the law (I was going to say the "biological" law) of the theological virtues, implanted by baptism deep in man's heart, to strain with all their dynamism toward their object, God. Faith aspires to an ever more perfect knowledge of the Lord, and charity yearns for an ever-closer union of love with him. And so grace, when it takes possession of a man, fills him with ravenous hunger and unquenchable thirst. The more grace grows within the soul, the more intense the hunger and thirst become.

And yet, I can't help thinking that you know these answers from Scripture and theology as well as I do. So you must be expecting something else from me. Am I mistaken in assuming that you are divided? That you wonder whether you should yield to the desire for God that inhabits you, or whether it isn't more perfect to yearn only for his glory?

Everyone who is progressing in the paths of prayer must face this choice sometime. Hesitancy in surrendering to the desire for union with God then stems from the sense that this desire is not totally pure. There is a fervent hope that this glimpse of God, which gives so much happiness, will be manifested again. But doesn't this desire contain more greed than generosity, more self-love than self-giving? One begins to wonder whether he must not resist it, so as to serve God with a disinterested love, free of self-seeking. Meanwhile, the desire is so tenacious and powerful that it wells up again and again.

There is no need to fear this desire. Rather, one should rejoice over it as a sure sign of the presence of the living God in the soul. The point is not to eliminate it, but to purify it. Anyway, God takes charge of this purification. The trek, through the desert and the darkness, will be so long that no self-love can survive it. On the other hand, the desire for God will grow deep within the soul. This time it will be wholly spiritual and pure, since it comes from God, is directed toward God, and is solely for the glory of God.

Does this mean that we must first reach a high degree of purification before we can dare confide to the Lord, during mental prayer, our irrepressible need to know him, love him, and be united to him? Of course not! A child should be simple and direct with his Father. He needs only to disavow any ambiguities in his desires.

We should not be afraid to express to God during mental prayer our desire for union with him. That is, provided that we are not merely sentimental *yearners* for him who scorn this action, but are indeed zealous *servants* of the Kingdom of Heaven.

In closing, allow me to copy for you a passage from the writings of St. Angela of Foligno. Once you have understood the distinctions I have just made, there is no danger of misinterpreting what she really meant.

* * *

The wise soul is not content to know God superficially, through reflection. It wants to know him in truth, savor his sovereign goodness and experience his infinity. Such a soul does not see God as merely a possession to be acquired, but as the supreme Good. It then loves him because of his goodness, and, loving him, it desires to possess him.

And God, in his great goodness, gives himself to the soul. Sensing this, the soul delights in his sweetness. Thus participating in the One who is sovereign love, the soul is enraptured with tenderness, and is united to God. . . . But the soul cannot attain such a lofty knowledge through its own efforts, through Scripture, through learning, or any created means, although these things can help and dispose toward it. Divine light and grace are needed for this.

Now, to obtain this favor quickly and surely, and to obtain it from God, the supreme Good, the supreme Light, the supreme Love, I know of no better way than devout, pure, unceasing petition. This is a petition that is both humble and vehement; a petition that is not uttered merely with the lips, but that springs from the mind, from the heart, from all the corporeal and spiritual faculties; a petition that wrests grace through its immense desire.

77. Begging from God

Y ou seem to be ashamed to address prayers of petition to God. Isn't this a subtle form of pride? Asking is the attitude of the beggar, offering is the attitude of generous and unselfish persons—and don't you want to be included among the latter?

And yet Christ has recommended the prayer of petition to us over and over again: *"Ask, and you will receive"* (Mt 7:7); *"your heavenly Father* [will] *give good things to anyone who asks him"* (Mt 7:11); *"whatever you ask in my name I will do"* (Jn 14:13); *"I tell you, if two of you join your voices on earth to pray for anything whatever, it shall be granted you by my Father in heaven"* (Mt 18:19).

In the face of Christ's insistence, how can anyone doubt that this prayer of petition is of the highest importance? Besides, it is easy to understand why. What could we offer to God, that we have not received from him? And how can we receive, if we do not hold out our hand? You dream of loving God in a selfless way. But how can you love him except with a love you have received from him? Left to your own resources, you are powerless to love God *"with your whole heart, with your whole soul, and with your whole mind"* (cf. Mt 22:37). You can truly love him only with the "new heart" that Ezekiel has promised in God's name: *"I will give you a new heart and place a new spirit within you, taking from your bodies your stony hearts and giving you natural hearts. I will put my Spirit within you"* (Ezk 36:26-27).

And that is precisely what we must pray for: that God may teach us to love, and give us the love with which to love him. I don't mean some tepid love, but the love that the New Testament writers express by the Greek word *agape*. This translates as "charity," a term that has become rather colorless in our modern parlance. Man is basically incapable of such love. It is divine in its origin and nature. It is the mutual love of the Father and the Son in the exultation of the Holy Spirit. It is also their love for men, magnificently manifested by the Father's gift of his Son, and by Christ's sacrifice of his life for our sakes.

"God is love" (1 Jn 4:16). This love is God's very nature. Outside of God this love can be found only in those whom he begets, that is, in those to whom he communicates his nature and his life. Then these beloved ones love God as he loves himself, and become his intimates and friends.

Do you understand this admirable teaching whose herald St. John became, after meditating on it during his long life? If you do, how can you fail to become the devotee of the prayer of petition? Sustained by indefectible faith and hope, you will beseech the Father to give you *agape*.

It is my fervent wish that you will be a beggar your whole life through. A beggar of *agape*. You must beg from God, whose riches will then become your very own.

78. The glory of God comes first

I never intended to imply that, in order to arrive at a more perfect mental prayer, one has to banish the prayer of petition. If my recent letter gave you such an idea, then I didn't express myself very well.

Regarding the sentiments of joy, fervor, and love, that you have often experienced during mental prayer, I was suggesting that you not ask for them and even renounce them insofar as it is God's good pleasure. In fact, we must learn how to renounce the sensible presence of God, to arrive at a more perfect intimacy with him. We must consent to the night, in order to emerge into the true light. Doesn't human love offer us an analogy? "Beloved, extinguish the lamp that does not allow me to see your face." Even though I advise you not to desire or ask for sensible graces, do not conclude that you are to abandon the prayer of petition.

Christ himself has taught us to ask the Father for what we need: our daily bread, forgiveness and protection. But he taught us to pray first that the Father's name be hallowed, that his Kingdom come and that his will be done. Yes indeed, the glory of God comes first. Not by a mere priority in time—as if, once we have prayed for the Kingdom of God, we have the right to petition for our own personal interests—but by an absolute priority. Our very petitions for bread, forgiveness and even for graces, must be made with God's glory in mind, and not primarily for our happiness or even for our salvation. We must pray that we may hallow his name through our whole life, so that in us and through us his Kingdom may come and his will be done. Seen in this light, prayer of petition is perfectly pure and truly great.

Returning to the matter of sensible graces, do not conclude, from what I have said, that you must dread or scorn them. The point is that you shouldn't engage in mental prayer for the sake of enjoying these graces, or imagine that fervor is better than pure faith. Once you understand this, be ready to welcome God's gifts with a simple and thankful heart. Learn to adapt yourself to abundance, as well as to famine. In the words of St. Benedict to his monks: "May God be glorified in all things!"

"Led by the Spirit of God"
(Rm 8:14)

The Holy Spirit is the teacher who shows us how to pray. He works in us to make us aware of our poverty and powerlessness. He teaches us to acquiesce in this, and thus prepares us to receive the graces that he will give.

Are those "wasted" periods of mental prayer, when we have the feeling of doing nothing, really time lost? Not at all! Rather, they are sacred. They are "the sacrifice of mental prayer."

79 *Place your offering on the rock*—When the Lord seems far away, it is time for us to reaffirm our faith in his present and active love. Then our desire grows deeper, and our love purer and more intense.

80 *Desert prayers*—If someone possesses everything except God, he has nothing; but nothing is lacking to the person stripped of everything except God. There is only one real poverty: being deprived of God.

81 *On that day, he will know how to pray*—Actually, God is never absent. He dwells within us. Even so, we must search for him where he is. We must listen attentively to the one whom we can hear clearly only amid silence.

82 *The legend of the musk deer*—Let us not speak, when deep within our souls we are invited to be silent, in an attitude of attention and self-offering.

83 *The kingdom of silence*—This interior silence and immobility are an extraordinarily intense activity. We must have no doubts about that.

84 *The invitation to silence*—In the mental prayer of silence, a child's heart gradually awakens within us. This is the child's heart which, according to Christ's own words, is qualified to enter the Kingdom of God.

85 *The captive girl-child*—The purified and silent soul soon discov-

ers, in its depths, light that penetrates the intellect and a love that strengthens the heart.

86   *Whiffs of prayer*—Such a soul's desire for God grows by leaps and bounds. But in the spiritual realm, "the soul's desire is satisfied by the very fact that it remains insatiable."

87   *Finding consists in seeking*—This desire becomes an irrepressible need to give God all the room within us, and surrender our whole substance to him, the way wood surrenders to the flame that consumes it.

79. Place your offering on the rock

Y ou write: "I feel I am wasting my time during mental prayer." Do you think it means nothing to waste your time, if you are really wasting it for God? We read in the Gospel: *"He who loses his life will find it"* (cf. Mt 10:39). Now, your time is the very fabric of your life. To "waste" or "lose" a fraction of it for God is, strictly speaking, to offer a sacrifice. Abel immolated a lamb from his flock, and his sacrifice was pleasing to God because he thereby acknowledged the Lord's supreme dominion over everything he possessed. You, for your part, are offering this hour of your day. You are destroying it, sacrificing it in the religious sense of the word. How can this "sacrifice of mental prayer" fail to be precious in the Lord's eyes, if through it you mean to affirm his supreme dominion over your whole life? Wasted time? Not at all. Rather, it is time that has been consecrated, made sacred.

You would probably prefer to have rapturous thoughts, fervor, or at the very least, genuine recollection, But then, might not your time of mental prayer become a search for your own personal satisfaction, rather than time consecrated to God?

When, during mental prayer, you are incapable of reflection, fervor and interior silence (in spite of your excellent intentions), then willingly acquiesce in this gift of a portion of your life. And banish all regret: that would amount to taking back with one hand what you are giving with the other.

You say that your mental prayer is of no use at all to you? Well then, it is truly the most excellent of sacrifices. It is a holocaust whose flames devour the victim to its last fibers, in contrast to a "sacrifice of communion," which involves the taking by the sacrificer of a portion of the sacrifice for his own use.

Your letter reached me as I was reading an intensely religious page of Scripture, which relates Gideon's sacrifice:

* * *

> *The angel of God said to him, "Take the meat and unleavened cakes and lay them on this rock; then pour out the broth." When he had done so, the angel of the Lord stretched out the top of the staff he held, and touched the meat and unleavened cakes. Thereupon a fire came up from the rock which consumed the meat and unleavened cakes, and the angel of the Lord disappeared from sight* (Jg 6:20-21).

* * *

When you come to mental prayer, place the offering of your time on the rock (St. Paul informs us that the Rock is Christ), and ask the angel of God to touch it with the tip of his staff. And then rejoice if the fire devours it, without leaving anything at all for you.

Is this to say that we should belittle the graces (silence, peace, joy, thoughts of a divine savor) that the Lord gives us during mental prayer? Of course not. If we knew how to be totally attentive to the Giver, rather than to the gifts received, the Holy Spirit would probably visit us even more frequently. But too often, God's gifts turn us away from him. So why be surprised that, out of love for us, God offers us famine rather than abundance? He doesn't want us to be satisfied with anything less than himself. And even so, how great is his impatience to satisfy us completely, by giving himself to us!

80. Desert prayers

Veronica is thirteen years old. Her mother taught her how to practice mental prayer very early in life, and she devotes ten or fifteen minutes to it each day. Last Sunday, in great distress, Veronica confided to me: "For the past week I have no longer experienced the presence of God."

* * *

My dear Veronica, I thought you would be glad to have in writing the advice I gave you the day before yesterday, especially since you have not yet recovered the presence of Christ in your daily mental prayer. For many months, he had been granting you the sense of his presence, and it felt very good. Now that this sense has been taken from you, you are all upset. I understand you, but don't worry. Don't tire yourself needlessly, trying to find out the reason for this change. Don't be too quick to think that it's your fault. Rather, strive to accept this trial willingly, good-naturedly, and with great patience. Little by little, you'll learn that these apparently sterile moments of mental prayer are very valuable. Christ's words to his disciples: *"It is much better for you that I go"* (Jn 16:7), will prove true for you also.

Your faith will emerge purer and stronger from this journey through the desert, where nothing grows and one never meets another human being. As long as Our Lord allowed you to sense his presence and his love, it was easy for you to cling to him, as the Apostles did when their risen Master appeared in their midst. But when no sensible sign comes to help your faith, it is forced to grow stronger and firmer. Remember Christ's words to Thomas: *"Blest are they who have not seen and have believed"* (Jn 20:29).

I invite you to strive very quietly and peacefully, during your desert prayers, to believe that Jesus is there, loving his little girl with a very great love. Nothing can give him greater glory than this firm faith.

Your interior life will reap a second considerable benefit from your toilsome mental prayer. Since you have become a boarding student, hasn't your desire to be with your family grown with each passing day? And isn't your return home all the more joyous, for having been so eagerly anticipated?

The same holds true for your times of mental prayer devoid of joy. Your desire to find Christ once more, and be more closely united to his love, will be intensified. That's essential, because as your desire intensifies, it will hollow out your soul more deeply, and you'll be able to offer Christ far more room to live within you. His grace will be given more abundantly to you, in the measure that you are more empty of self, and more eager to receive him. This eagerness is the virtue of hope.

There's a third benefit, too. Your love for Christ, like metal in the furnace, is purified in these purgatorial times of mental prayer. Didn't you often go to mental prayer eager to find the joy you had experienced the day before? That might indicate that you were not going to mental prayer solely to please God, but also out of a certain self-love.

When we become aware of this, we should be the first to tell our Lord: "I want to get rid of this old self-love, and go to mental prayer, not for the joy it gives me, but only for your glory. And so I beg you to keep me from finding joy in it, as long as necessary." Even if we do not take the initiative, let us at least accept, patiently and peacefully, the denial to us of the joys of mental prayer.

Above all, don't be like those who spend their entire period of mental prayer eagerly watching for the return of joy. Such people make me think of children who hardly sleep a wink on Christmas Eve, because they're watching for the arrival of toys under the Christmas tree. I hope the day will come when you will even be happy when your mental prayer is devoid of joy. Then you'll know that you love Jesus a little more than you love yourself.

Wasn't I right, Veronica, in telling you that your desert prayers are very useful? In this kind of prayer, the three great virtues are purified and perfected: faith, hope and charity. These are precisely the virtues that put us in contact with our God, and initiate us into his own divine life.

81. On that day, he will know how to pray

A mother wrote to me: "I had gone into my little son's room, to kiss him good night before he went to sleep. I put out the light and was about to leave, when he begged me in a distressed tone of voice: 'Mommy, don't go!' I turned back and bent down over him: 'Why, dear?' 'Because when you're not there, I'm . . . I'm . . . poor.'"

In my answer to her, I wrote:

I don't know when a child's words have made such a deep impression on me. Your Philip's words have stayed with me ever since I read them. He could have said: "I'm sad," or even, "I'm afraid!" That would have been quite usual. Besides, sadness and fear quickly vanish. But, after searching for the word that was exactly right to express what he really felt, he said: "I'm poor." That means so much more. A poor person is someone who lacks necessities, who needs bread and may die if he doesn't get it. That's just what your little boy felt so intensely that night. His Mom was his daily bread, his reason for living. Without her, he was poor to the point of anguish.

May the day come, when he will be able to say to God with the same vigor and conviction, "Lord, don't go away! Because when you're not there, I'm poor." On that day, he will know how to pray.

82. The legend of the musk deer

W hy exhaust yourself searching for God, as if he were outside of you? He is within you. That's where he has made a rendezvous with you, and is waiting for you. And that's where he'll allow you to find him in his own good time.

Hindu mothers tell their children the legend of the musk deer, to make them understand this great truth:

* * *

"One day many years ago, the musk deer of the mountains sniffed a breath of musked perfume. He leaped from jungle to jungle in pursuit of the musk. The poor animal no longer ate, or drank, or slept. He didn't know where the scent of the musk came from, but he was impelled to pursue it through ravines, forests and hills. Finally, starving, harassed, exhausted and wandering about at random, he slipped from the top of a rock and fell mortally wounded.

"The musk deer's last act before he died was to take pity on himself and lick his breast. And his musk pouch, torn when he fell on the rock, poured out its perfume. He gasped and tried to breathe in the perfume, but it was too late. Beloved son, don't seek the perfume of God outside yourself, and perish in the jungle of life. Search your soul and look within. He will be there."

* * *

The God within you is not a silent God. And yet, if we want to hear him, we must be silent. "The Father speaks one Word, and this Word is his Son. He speaks his Word in eternal silence, and it is in silence that the soul hears him" (St. John of the Cross).

It's hard to create silence in our frightfully noisy world. I am speaking not only of perceptible sounds, but also of all the events, sensational news, and various messages, that the communications media shout out over the rooftops and hiss into our ears. All this commotion perturbs our senses, our imagination, our thinking, and our heart. It dances a wild saraband within us, disrupting our prayer life. Nonetheless, interior silence is still possible.

To achieve this silence, we must practice it patiently and gently. Violent means have never been a way to pacification. We are speaking of the pacification of all our faculties, so that they may become receptive to God, motionless and at attention. This last term evokes a certain quality of silence: recollection. It is an attention that is completely alert, listening eagerly for the interior voice. Claudel wrote:

* * *

"Many wise men had already told us that in order to hear, it was perhaps enough for us to listen. How true! But now it is not with our auditory apparatus, it is not even with our straining intellect, that we keep watch. It is our whole being that listens to Being live."

* * *

You'll probably tell me once again, that you despair of attaining to interior silence, to sacred recollection. True, your own unaided efforts cannot suffice for this. Divine grace must intervene. But how can God refuse this grace? He is much too anxious to see silence established in your soul, so that dialogue can begin between the Father and his child.

Trust and persevere in mental prayer. Christ will pacify your vagrant faculties and bring them back to himself, like the shepherd St. Teresa of Avila tells about, who plays his reed pipe at dusk to gather his sheep scattered over the meadows.

83. The kingdom of silence

It's up to you rather than me, to know whether you should give up the form of active mental prayer that you have followed until now, and turn to a more passive form of prayer. In any event, here are a few elements on which to make a judgment.

Let us suppose that during mental prayer you are inclined to remain silent and immobile, close to the God whom you do not see, but whom you are sure is there. Words seem superfluous, far less explicit and true than the silence of your being, offered to the Lord's gaze. After concluding your mental prayer, you are at peace, and as though renewed. Then search no further. The Holy Spirit has introduced you into the kingdom of silence.

But don't expect this kingdom to be an earthly paradise. There will be times when you'll need great courage to resist the temptation to flee from this austere and desert land. At such times, may your strength lie in the Lord's promise recorded in the small book of the prophet Hosea: "*I will lead* [him] *into the desert and speak to* [his] *heart*" (Ho 2:16).

Be on your guard against the contrary temptation to cling to this new form of prayer, fearing that you will retrogress if you turn back. There will indeed be days when silence would be empty, when you would be wasting your time if you were not active. At such times, return in all humility to the mental prayer you know well. This consists in thinking about God, in letting him speak, and in asking him to bless those whom you encounter and the tasks you have to carry out.

There may be times when you are unsure as to what you ought to do. It will seem as if your innermost soul is alert and attentive to God, in a zone impervious to noise. Meanwhile in your soul's periphery, emotions, passions, thoughts and sensations will be running wild. Don't be disturbed, but follow your innermost soul. As for everything else, all that is churning about and demanding your attention, respond with indifference and rejection. To reject something is to render it harmless.

84. The invitation to silence

I shall not hide from you that I was somewhat disconcerted by the question you asked in your last letter: "When we do nothing at all during mental prayer, how can we be sure that this is really what God wants?" I was going to answer: "It's never God's will that we do nothing during mental prayer, because all true mental prayer is essentially an activity." But as I was not prepared to receive rash questions from you, I tried to figure out the exact meaning of your request. Tell me if I have understood you correctly.

There are times during mental prayer when we are absent in spirit.

After a few minutes, we are surprised to find ourselves kneeling, and notice that our mind's activity has not been interrupted. The interior film strip has continued to roll. At other times, after a good start in mental prayer, we catch ourselves thinking of all sorts of things foreign to our prayer, or else our mind seems to be floating on a cloud of peaceful lethargy. Are you referring to states of soul such as these? If so (but I doubt it), it is quite obvious that you need to regain control of your thoughts. You must turn your attention back to God, search for a faith-filled thought and dwell on it, and make an effort to love God.

I am inclined to think that your question concerns moments when, during mental prayer, we no longer want to reflect on a specific subject, or even make distinct acts of adoration, praise, and love. These are moments when we feel impelled to interior immobility and silence. A certain anxiety, however, keeps us from surrendering unreservedly to this impulsion. Is this authentic mental prayer?

Here is my advice to you. If you sense that interior silence is more authentic, and that it absorbs you more deeply than words, then do not hesitate to opt for silence. Above all, reject the temptation to think that this means you are inactive. In the deepest recesses of your being, there is activity going on—delicate, subtle, very pure and scarcely perceptible because it is very spiritual. It is a turning toward God of your innermost self, an activity that is far more real and true than effervescing feelings or imaginings, than the most elating thoughts or sentiments. This activity is divine, elicited within you by the Spirit of the Lord. These moments filled with silence (there are empty silences as well) are among the privileged moments of mental prayer.

But take heed! Do not try to bring on these moments. You cannot attain to this state of soul, or maintain yourself in it, through your own efforts. It is a matter of grace. When you do not feel this inclination to silence within yourself, simply go back to your former form of mental prayer. Think about God, speak to him, love him, and offer yourself to him. But be ready to quit all these activities, the instant the Holy Spirit invites you to silence once more.

85. The captive girl-child

A pastor had invited me to preach the Holy Week services in his mountain village. In administering the sacrament of reconciliation to his parishioners, I discovered that quite a few of them had a spiritual formation of rare quality. There was a family resemblance among these souls. Their relations with God were filled with filial trust, peace, and cheerful generosity. I concluded that under his rough mountaineer exterior, the pastor concealed an extraordinary interior life, and was an awakener of souls.

However, our conversations at meals and during the evening were very disappointing, restricted to very general theological and pastoral problems. I refused to be satisfied with this, and obstinately tried to reach the wellspring through the brambles.

On Easter day, both at the Masses and at Vespers, a vibrant and controlled fervor was clearly perceptible in the assembled parish community. At supper that evening, a deep inner joy emanated from the pastor's austere countenance. And yet, our final conversation was about to assume the impersonal tone of the earlier ones. A comment on my part, however, turned our talk in an unexpected direction, allowing me a glimpse into a singularly profound priestly soul. I recently came across the few notes I scribbled down after returning to my room that Easter night. I am sending them to you. They are a faithful, if not complete, record of the good pastor's remarks.

* * *

"For so many people, the Christian life is synonymous with effort, tension, contention, performance, records. [To stress and give nuances to his thought, the pastor seemed to take pleasure in this accumulation of words.] But it is really much less muscular, visible, external. It is something in the depths of one's being, something tenuous, delicate, subtle, relaxed, an act of the soul, an acquiescence of our interior freedom.

"Below, far below our religious acts, our clumsy generosities, our sensible fervors, our vehement desires, and our short-winded aspirations, there lies within us a zone of freshness, innocence, virginity. The harshnesses, anxieties, meannesses, and impurities of life cannot touch it, pollute it, contaminate it. That is where our child's soul lives—young, fresh, pure, intact, inviolate. But among practically all people, the girl-child is shut away.

"To be a Christian is first of all to liberate the captive girl-child, to bring her to the light, to untie her fetters. And then she breathes and begins to sing a limpid, crystalline song.

How I wish we could cry out to so many church-going men and women:

* * *

'You'll never get to heaven with your self-important airs, your moralistic reasoning, your stuffy virtues, your spiritual bookkeeping and spiritual investments. You'll be obliged to throw all that overboard. But with the soul of a child, yes. Led by this little girl-child, if you consent to take her by the hand, you will enter the kingdom of heaven reserved for young children and for those who resemble them.

'It never ceases to astonish you—and no doubt to scandalize you in secret—that Christ promised heaven at so small a price to the public sinner, to the adulterous wife, to the thief who hung on the cross next to him. The reason is, that when they came into contact with him, the child-soul of each of them was suddenly liberated, and murmured this very simple word, this word of love, this "Yes!" that orientates a destiny.'

* * *

"It's really so simple to be saved—but that's just it! One must consent to its being simple. Our eternal destiny unfolds not at the level of edifying actions, conformist virtues, or great undertakings, but within the innermost recesses of the soul. It seems to be only a breath, a modulation. It seems insignificant, but in fact nothing is more powerful, more efficacious. Our eternity is decided by a certain childlike smile of our soul—candid, pure, trusting, boldly confident. That's it. I think a certain unique quality of smile wrested the Son of God from the Trinitarian Life, and drew him irresistibly into the womb of a young girl named Mary."

* * *

Then I asked my pastor-friend, "How can we recover our child-soul and restore its gusto for life, for song and for smiles?"

"I know of nothing more effective than mental prayer," was his answer. "Provided, of course, that the adult stops talking, and becomes the pupil of the emancipated girl-child. But if we were to make inquiries. . . ."

With that the speaker definitively closed our conversation, which I was so eager to prolong.

86. Whiffs of prayer

Don't imagine that you are one of a kind. Many others go through the same experiences as you. A physician-friend of mine said to me recently, "Often when I am driving my car, or am between patients, I feel impelled to pray. At such times, I look forward to the moment when I can enter a church. But when at last I am there, the prayer that I had thought was ready to well up is gone from my mind." Many a mother has confided to me that her periods of mental prayer remain desperately dry, but that she can pray without any difficulty while cleaning the house or preparing the meals.

Several explanations can probably be given for this common occurrence. Before proposing a good explanation, I invite you to broaden and deepen your perspective.

The Blessed Trinity lives within us. According to Christ's promise to his Apostles, *"Anyone who loves me will be true to my word, and my Father will love him; we will come to him and make our dwelling place with him"* (Jn 14:23).

The Trinity is not within us the way, for example, that a host is in a ciborium. Rather, it is present in the way that fire is present in the log it is consuming, or the way that the soul lives in the body. I make these comparisons to help you understand that, in prayer, we are united to the very life of the Triune God. Our innermost being, that most secret area of ourselves (and the one we know least), shares in the Trinitarian life. Superficial as we may be, we sometimes receive, from this center of our soul, messages, mysterious admonitions and invitations to recollection. To be recollected means to redirect our attention away from our external concerns, and to become receptive to interior realities.

If we accept the invitation, put everything else aside, and listen attentively, our innermost life often comes to the surface of our consciousness. More precisely, we penetrate into this interior world that we—perennially distracted beings—neglect to cultivate.

"But," you may point out, "it is precisely when I am answering what I think is a call from God, and turn to mental prayer, that I don't perceive anything or feel any need to pray. In short, I feel that I'm bored."

Is the reason, perhaps, that your intellect is striving to produce ideas, and your heart is laboring to produce feelings, at a time when you should be totally immobile and receptive? Please understand that, in order to know and love God more, it is often better to be receptive than active. Think of those ponds that are fed from within. The same is true of your soul. Your intellect is there within you, capable of receiving the light of the Word. If it is open, then, the light will shine forth within its center and spread through it. Ready your heart likewise, to receive from within the Trinitarian love. This is the charity that wants to fill and dilate it, so that it can overflow onto others.

I am not saying that we must always adopt this passive attitude during mental prayer. I even refrain from advising it to beginners. It is proper for them to fill the pond by drawing from outside, by nourishing their minds and hearts with the Word of God. That's the way to begin and to continue, perhaps for many long years. It's necessary as long as infused contemplation, as the theologians call it, has not welled up from within.

Even so, we must be alert. This infused contemplation does not offer our intellect distinct ideas, and does not necessarily arouse expressible sentiments. It runs the risk, at least in the early stages, of passing unnoticed.

It is precisely because this contemplation is divine, that it overflows and foils our human modes of thinking and loving.

Have I wandered from my subject? Not at all. These "whiffs of prayer," that come when you are not trying to pray, are probably an invitation to a greater passivity before God, to greater interior flexibility and docility. In this way, the Holy Spirit can communicate his divine impulses to your pacified and receptive soul, and initiate you into infused contemplation.

So learn not to seek on the outside, what is within you. Stop trying to produce what you are meant to receive.

87. Finding consists in seeking

T his letter was addressed to a young priest who, after several years of
parish ministry, obtained permission from his bishop to retire in
solitude to lead a life of prayer and penance.

* * *

I wonder if your desire, to know God and be united to him, does not
involve excessive tension that threatens to destroy you. The path to
holiness is long and hard. It will require all the resources that you can
muster. The spiritual combat is implacable, and you'll need every ounce
of your strength to succeed.

This desire for God, that has led you into solitude, is certainly a
great grace. You must value this desire and nurture it. But it is just as
important to channel and purify it. God will respond not so much to its
vehemence, as to its purity.

Such a desire is often mixed with an alloy of fantasy and spiritual
greed. There is a tendency to yearn for the day when, this desire at last
satisfied, we can rest in the possession of God right here on earth. That
is a delusion.

With God, it is not the same as with temporal riches. The possession
of the latter extinguishes desire *ipso facto*. In contrast, the more we
possess God the more we desire him, and the more actively we seek him.

Earthly things are limited, and can be wholly possessed: a table or a
house, for example. They satisfy our desire. But God, the Infinite One,
exceeds us in every way. The more we know, love, and possess God, the
more evident it is that he can be known, loved, and possessed far more
completely. Our desire for him is always welling up anew.

We should be delighted to have this desire. At the root of our being,
it is God's thought penetrating our intellect. He is forcing it to enlarge
its capacity, so that he can communicate himself to it more fully. It is
God pressing on our heart, so that he can give his love to us more
perfectly. God is thus within us, knowing and loving himself. He wants
to make us share in his living knowledge and love of himself. That is the
reason for this desire to know and love God, that permeates the souls of
his friends.

You are impatient for more perfect union with God. How could it be
otherwise? But be patiently impatient. Realize that your desire (although it cannot be satisfied on earth) will be progressively more fully

satisfied and more intense, in the measure that you come closer to God.

St. Gregory of Nyssa based his whole spirituality on the following affirmation: "Finding God consists in seeking him incessantly." And he explains what he means:

* * *

"Indeed, seeking and finding are not two distinct acts. For success in seeking consists in the search itself. The soul's desire is satisfied by the very fact that it remains insatiable. For truly seeing God consists in never being satiated with desiring him."

* * *

Are you going to object, "But then, when shall we ever find rest?" You will find less and less, as you approach God. Just as the speed of a falling stone accelerates as it plunges downward, so, too, the soul's upward flight intensifies the closer it comes to God.

There is no worse mistake than to consider perfection, in our earthly condition, as a repose of desire in the stable possession of God. To the contrary, it is an active search, movement, and aspiration toward him. Quoting again from St. Gregory of Nyssa:

* * *

"Because of the transcendence of the riches the soul discovers, in the measure that it progresses, it always seem to be only at the start of its ascent. That is why the Word repeats "Arise!" to the soul that is already awake, and "Come!" to the one that has already come. In truth, the one who is really arising must always continue to arise, and the one who runs toward the Lord will never lack much space in which to run. And so the one who is ascending never stops, proceeding from beginning to beginning through beginnings that never end."*

* For more information on the mystical teachings of St. Gregory of Nyssa, consult the following:
From Glory to Glory: Texts From Gregory of Nyssa's Mystical Writings
Selected and with an Introduction by Jean Danielou, S.J.
Translated and Edited by Herbert Musurillo, S.J.
Charles Scribner's Sons, 1961, St. Vladimir's Seminary Press, 1979.
The Life of Moses, by Gregory of Nyssa.
Translation, Introduction and Notes by Abraham J. Malherbe and Everett Ferguson. Paulist Press, 1978.

"... whoever is joined to the Lord becomes one spirit with him" (1 Cor 6:17)

Our desire to find God, that led us to mental prayer, did not lie. The eagerly desired union becomes a reality close at hand, deep within us.

To find God! This is what we must expect of mental prayer, and this is what it holds out for us.

88   *I want to learn how to pray*—Mental prayer is indeed a holy place where God speaks to man's heart, and embraces him with his powerful and tender love.

89   *Meditation before a portrait*—God does not wait until the end of a life of mental prayer, to manifest his active presence in a praying soul. Sometimes he manifests himself very early. Mystical experience is not reserved for the saints alone. Those who discredit it are to be pitied, and even more those to whom it is offered, and who spurn it.

90   *Mysticism*—The person to whom mystical experience is offered, sees clearly that mental prayer consists less in "doing" than in "being." This means being with God, attentive to him present in the soul.

91   *To be or to act*—Unquestionably, asceticism is needed to arrive at this experience. The converse is still truer: the mystical graces are powerful helps in the practice of the virtues. They enable our love for God to free itself gradually from our love of self.

92   *Said*—The mystical graces cause a mysterious knowledge of the Lord to burgeon within us, provided, of course, that our intellect humbles itself before "the lofty incomprehensibility of God."

93   *"You will see my back"* (cf. Ex 33:23)—The mystical graces are active in uniting us to God. This union consists essentially in the fusion of our innermost will with the will of God.

94   *The mental prayer of a woman of the people*—The stages on this road toward union with God are not the same for everyone, but progress always involves the development of a more ardent and selfless love.

95   *Beacons along the road*—In any event, the union will not be consummated until we have yielded all the room within us to God.

96   *It's you*—When that day comes, we shall be introduced into the communion of love between the Father and the Son, that eternal feast whose bard and witness, in heaven and on earth, is the Holy Spirit.

97   *"God's rest"* (Heb 4:10).

88. I want to learn how to pray

Y ou say, "I would like to know how to pray." Thank God for this wish! It can only come from him. Even so, you must ask yourself why you want to learn to pray.

An old French story will explain my thinking to you better than a long discourse.

* * *

In ancient times, there were many hermits living in the forests of the Vosges Mountains. One of them had a great reputation for holiness. Hunters claimed that they had seen wild animals—bears, wild boars, roe deer—gathered and as though recollected before the entrance of his cave, while he sang the Lord's praises. The inhabitants of the valley were no longer surprised, when they noticed a strange glow in the sky at night above the mountain where the man of God lived.

Quite often, young men of the region asked him to take them in. Didn't other hermits live with disciples whom they initiated into contemplation? But they all received the same negative answer. All but one. This privileged young man revealed the reason for his good fortune, shortly after his master's death.

* * *

"When I was eighteen years old I presented myself, and requested the favor of dwelling close to him. When he asked me why, I answered, 'Because I want to learn how to pray.' These words kindled a gleam of tenderness in the old hermit's eyes. Then he asked me, 'And why do you want to learn to pray?' 'Because that is the loftiest knowledge.' 'I would like very much to take you in, but I can't,' he answered with some sadness.

"I returned to see him three years later. He received me with a father's affection, and again asked me, 'Why do you want to learn how to pray?' 'So I can become a saint.' I was convinced that this time, he would accept me. Wasn't this the loftiest conceivable reason? But once again he refused, and I left in despair.

"I went back to work in the fields. And yet the desire to pray haunted me more than ever, from morning until night. Sometimes I would weep, when I thought of the man who lived up there on the mountain, in intimate friendship with his God.

"One Christmas Eve, I suddenly got up. I was absolutely sure that this time, he would accept me. When I arrived, he was praying and didn't notice me. I waited a long time. Gradually, my impatience quieted down. When he turned around, he didn't seem at all surprised by my presence. I began to speak, without giving him time to ask any questions. 'I want to learn how to pray *because I want to find God.*' Then he opened his arms and welcomed me."

* * *

To find God is the purpose of true prayer. It makes prayer irresistible. The Father cannot turn away from the child who is seeking him. The child finally understands that he must no longer run from the Father who is pursuing him.

What does it mean to find God? Grace gradually causes this need to mature in the Christian heart. Those who have found God would love to disclose their secret to us, but they are up against an impossible obstacle. Neither words nor concepts can express the intimacy of the soul with its God. They are reduced to assuring us that the path of prayer is not a blind alley. It opens up into a great meadow, and culminates in an ineffable, divine experience.

89. Meditation before a portrait

D o you remember the page of the Bible where Moses is tending his sheep on the slopes of Horeb, and stops before a bush that is burning without being consumed? He trembles with a sacred fear. Then he steps forward to observe the prodigy, but a voice rises from the flames that stops him in his tracks: *"Come no nearer! Remove the sandals from your feet, for the place where you stand is holy ground"* (Ex 3:5).

Prayer is a sacred place, the holy ground where God dwells. There he waits for man, speaks to him, and embraces him with his strong and tender love.

Since prayer is God's activity even more than man's, it is at least partly beyond the scope of rational inquiry. It is a mystery. However, we are certainly permitted to seek to understand prayer better. That is even one of the loftiest goals of the human intellect. But to succeed, we must renounce all hope of wresting its ultimate secret. Rather, we must follow the guidance of the Holy Spirit and advance humbly, in our bare feet.

I cannot hope to convince you of the importance of prayer, as long as you persist in being an "old rationalist," refusing to rise above the level of philosophy.

At your next visit, I shall show you a painting of Benedict-Joseph Labre, the beggar saint. Perhaps this picture will be more convincing than my arguments. It has always made a deep impression on me. I find it extraordinarily moving. It represents the saint at prayer, his arms folded, his head slightly bowed, and his eyelids lowered. There is a feeling of intense recollection. Benedict-Joseph Labre is a total stranger to the world around him. He is completely centered within himself, with the doors of his senses carefully closed. What is going on within this private sanctuary? Obviously, that is beyond the reach of our eyes.

Even so, looking at this picture, we can glimpse the saint's secret. There is an indefinable halo of tenderness and humility that envelops his person, and a light that seems to illumine his face from within. There can be no doubt that this man's heart is experiencing something very important and enviable. We are impelled to kneel before Benedict-Joseph at prayer, because we are certain that the God who lives in his soul is speaking words to him that make him blessed, words very sweet to hear.

This picture taught me much more about prayer than reading many books. Perhaps it will speak to you, too.

90. Mysticism

M y dear Father, I cannot hide from you that last Wednesday evening I was astonished—to put it mildly—at the indifferent tone,
bordering on ridicule, with which you spoke of mysticism and mystics. I
felt that it was a kind of profanation. I thought of our great Catholic
saints, most of whom, we know, were mystics. As I watched these
students listen with such trust to their young chaplain, I felt there was a
danger that you might disorient some of those who were aspiring to an
encounter with God. In listening to you, they could be led to despair of
finding God in a Catholic religion where everything was reduced to
rational explanations, and to a morality of action.

The infatuation of certain young people and famous writers with
the religions of India, the success of various cults and the unbelievable
prestige enjoyed in Paris by some seer from the Orient, often have no
other explanation than the disparagement of the mystical life by so
many Catholic priests and lay people. Do not retort that, sooner or
later, every confessor has had a bone to pick with false mystics. I am well
aware of that. But do false Rembrandts necessarily discredit the authentic works of the Dutch Master?

It goes without saying that we must distinguish between genuine
and false mystics, and correctly define the word whose real meaning is
so often distorted! Passing over subtleties, I shall say that the true mystic
perceives the active presence of God at "the center of his soul," and
receives various inspirations from this presence—to prayer, love, action
and self-sacrifice. Like St. Paul, he can say: *"The Spirit himself gives witness
with our spirit that we are children of God"* (Rm 8:16).

St. Paul reveals himself to be a great mystic on every page of his
Epistles. He is aware of being caught up by the power of God, of being
led by his Spirit. He declares to us that this is the hallmark of the
children of God: *"All who are led by the Spirit of God are sons of God"* (Rm
8:14).

You see that I am not including, in the definition of mystical experience, various "extraordinary" phenomena: ecstasies, visions and revelations. They can occur in an authentic mystical life, but they are not
what essentially constitutes this life.

You may object: "Mysticism is the consecration of holiness. What's the use of talking about it to those who are plodding along in the valleys?" No, mystical experience is not reserved for the saints. It plays a part (at least in the form of transitory graces) in the onset of many conversions, as well as in the lives of beginners on the path to holiness. I agree, of course, that the summits of mystical experience are reached only by those who are very advanced in the spiritual life. Such persons live with God, by God, and in God.

St. John of the Cross has described the innermost life of the great mystics in his *Ascent Of Mount Carmel*:

> "In thus allowing God to work in it, the soul . . . is at once illumined and transformed in God, and God communicates to it His supernatural Being, in such wise that it appears to be God Himself, and has all that God himself has.
>
> . . . all the things of God and the soul are one in participant transformation; and the soul seems to be God rather than a soul, and is indeed God by participation; although it is true that its natural being, though thus transformed, is as distinct from the Being of God as it was before, even as the window has likewise a nature distinct from that of the ray, though the ray gives it brightness."*

The beginner is indeed far from such an experience. However, the Lord sometimes allows him to glimpse these summits, to spur him on to desire and pursue union with God, the goal of every Christian life. St. Teresa of Avila and St. Jane de Chantal relate that their young nuns very often attained to a mystical mental prayer after six months or a year in the novitiate.

Mystical experience, as the definition I gave you earlier implied, is not limited to times of formal mental prayer. In the midst of action, the mystic experiences the fact that he is led by God. He is led to act, or led to pray while he is acting. However, it is during formal mental prayer that the soul discovers more readily that its God is within, present and acting. The reason for this is simply that, at that particular time, the soul

---

* *Ascent Of Mount Carmel*, Book 2, Chapter 5, Paragraph 7 in volume one of *The Complete Works of St. John of the Cross*, translated and edited by E. Allison Peers, Newman Press, 1935, 1964.

makes a conscious effort to be completely free, available, and surrendered to God. Again, I shall borrow the description of this experience from St. John of the Cross.

He first calls to mind that, in its early phase, mental prayer consists
in meditating. He then shows that prayerful souls, especially if they
have given up everything to surrender themselves to God in the religious life, soon receive the grace of "infused contemplation." This is the
way he describes this new form of mystical mental prayer:

* * *

"For God secretly and quietly infuses into the soul loving
knowledge and wisdom without any intervention of specific acts,
although sometimes He specifically produces them in the soul for
some length of time. And the soul has then to walk with loving
advertence to God, without making specific acts, but conducting
itself, as we have said, passively, and making no efforts of its own,
but preserving this simple, pure and loving advertence, like one
that opens his eyes with the advertence of love.

Since God, then, as giver, is communing with the soul by
means of loving and simple knowledge, the soul must likewise
commune with Him by receiving with a loving and simple
knowledge or advertence, so that knowledge may be united with
knowledge and love with love. For it is meet that he who receives
should behave in conformity with that which he receives, and not
otherwise, in order to be able to receive and retain it as it is given to
him . . ."*

* * *

Let no one imagine that this is some sort of luxurious pastime.
During mental prayer such as this, God works great things within the
soul, and consequently great things in the Church:

* * *

---

* *Living Flame of Love*, Stanza 3, Paragraphs 31 and 32, in volume three of *The
Complete Works*.

And the smallest part of this that God brings to pass in the soul in holy rest and solitude is an inestimable blessing, greater sometimes than either the soul itself, or he that guides it, can imagine. . . .*

To dissuade the soul from this form of prayer, from this "supernatural recollection," "to bring it out of the gulf of deep water," as some spiritual directors sometimes do, is—St. John of the Cross vigorously declares—a sin whose consequences are incalculable:

> ". . . it is a thing of no small weight, and no slight crime, to cause the soul to lose inestimable blessings by counselling it to go out of its way and to leave it prostrate. . . .
> "For the business of God has to be undertaken with great circumspection, and with eyes wide open, most of all in matters so delicate and sublime as the conduct of these souls, where a man may bring them almost infinite gain if the advice that he gives be good and almost infinite loss if it be mistaken."**

* * *

Does this mean that such a life of mental prayer is one of complete repose, without trials, dangers, or illusions? Of course not. That's why St. John of the Cross, St. Teresa, and so many others set out, in their writings, to guide the souls that God is leading along this path.

Need we fear lest this life of mental prayer draw lay persons away from the apostolate? The example of St. Teresa of Avila suffices to refute this objection. The more a soul commits itself to the path of mental prayer, the stronger and more intense within it becomes the need to know and make known, to love and make others love, and to serve and inspire others to serve the Lord. To quote Bergson:

* * *

---

* *Living Flame of Love* (second redaction), Stanza 3, Paragraph 39, in volume three of *The Complete Works*.

** *Living Flame of Love*, Stanza 3, Paragraph 48, in volume three of *The Complete Works*.

"It's an irresistible impulsion that plunges it into vast under-takings. A calm exaltation of all its faculties gives it far-ranging vision, and weak as it may be, makes it accomplish great things. Above all, it sees things simply, and this simplicity, which is evident both in its words and in its behavior, guides it through complications that it doesn't even seem to notice. An innate knowledge, or rather an acquired innocence, thus suggests from the start the useful course, the decisive action, the unanswerable word. Withal, effort remains indispensable, as well as endurance and perseverance. But these come of their own accord. They unfold spontaneously in the soul that is both acting and 'acted upon,' whose liberty coincides with the activity of God."

***

Forgive me, dear Father, for writing to you at such length. But this subject is particularly important to me. I observe that the Christian life of those who surrender to the guidance of the Spirit of God, is so much more vital! They manifest great joy of soul, even amid trials. They persevere in their ascent toward God, even if they sometimes grow faint on the way, and their actions reveal exceptional power and efficacy.

May you see this letter, dear Father, as the sign of my very great esteem for your priestly dedication, and of my hope that you may lead the many souls that place their trust in you, to the closest possible union with God.

Please believe in my fraternal friendship.

91. To be or to act?

During our last visit, I told you that Christian prayer is not merely a human activity. Rather, it springs from the depths of our "Christian being," that *"shares in the divine nature"* (cf. 2 P 1:4). And as you probably remember, I added, "Don't pray with your human intellect or emotions. Pray with your innermost being."

As it happens, this "prayer of one's being" is evoked in a letter I have just received. I am copying a passage from it for you. As you will see, it is not written in a Christian climate. A certain pantheistic mentality seems to pervade it. That doesn't prevent the advice that my correspondent received from being understood in a sense acceptable to a Christian. And now here's the letter:

* * *

During a business trip around the world, I had the opportunity to spend a few days in India. My mind was still full of the things I had read many years before, about this prestigious land. And so I asked my French friends who were offering me hospitality, and who had lived in India many years, whether there were still any of those "holy men," permeated with wisdom and prayer, whose influence had been so great in India over the centuries.

Actually, this was not the world in which my friends lived. Anyway, being anxious to please me, they made inquiries. And one day they brought me into a small, remote village, and left me at the house of a "holy man." They had been told that he had great renown throughout the region.

The man, who received me in a kind of a hut, was about seventy years old. Poor, thin, and wearing only a loincloth, he gave the appearance of great moral strength and purity of soul.

I told him in my halting English that I was a Catholic, but didn't want to leave India without being counseled by a wise man, rich in the religious traditions of the country. What a surprise for me to learn that he was British! For many years he had practiced medicine in this distant land. For the past fifteen years, he has spent his life in prayer, and in teaching the ways of prayer to those who come to him. His spirituality seemed rather offbeat, but deeply religious.

He looked at me for a long time. I wondered if he had understood me. I was almost embarrassed by his gaze—clear, insistent, and penetrating, but also very kindly.

At last, he began to question me. "Do you pray every day?" "Yes," I answered, "but only for a short while." "And how do you pray?" I described my method of mental prayer: adoration, reflection on a page of Scripture, then praise, and finally petitions for myself and for others.

He smiled as he listened to me. It was a smile full of sympathy, but, seemingly, not free from a certain condescension.

He went on to say, "Westerners always think that to pray is to *do* something. Here, all the sages have taught us that to pray is to *be*. If there is being, of what use is the added doing? If there is no being, then the doing is devoid of value." Seeing that I didn't understand his thought at first, he explained.

* * *

"To pray is to be. I am not speaking of activities or attitudes of the mind. Being is the substance of man. This is what we must bring to God. We must be there, attentive to God, with him, for him, and in his presence, stripped of all having and all doing. Being is the only true action, the action that is intense, surging, irrepressible, efficacious, and powerful.

"It isn't easy to be. Our being is covered over with the sediments of non-being. We must begin by freeing ourselves from them. Our being must be revitalized. Then it must be exposed naked to the rays of divinity. Then perhaps, some day, it will be drawn in by the Great Being, like the drop of dew that evaporates in the sunshine and goes to join the clouds.

"On that day, to be will consist in being in the One who is, being in God, being God."

* * *

Turning to me, the "holy man" asked, "Do you want to pray for a moment with me?" And seated on the bare earth in the Buddha position, my host recollected himself, or rather was seized by recollection. All at once, I felt he was miles away from me. I couldn't pray. I couldn't take my eyes off his face, which was becoming more beautiful with each passing minute, as though transparent to a light within him.

Time slipped by unnoticed. At nightfall, I withdrew without making the slightest noise. But he opened his eyes and looked at me with great love: "From now on when you pray to your God, we shall be side by side just as we were today, more perfectly than today."

92. Said

My dear Jacques, you are right in thinking that to become a man of prayer, one must discipline his instincts, put order in his priorities, and attain interior unity. Does this mean that before beginning the practice of mental prayer, one must have attained perfect self-mastery? I am less convinced of this than you. But before presenting my point of view, I'd like you to read the letter a friend sent me twenty years ago, and that I recently found. I am copying it down for you:

* * *

"Here I am again, after many long years of absence in this North African city I love so much. There is the joy of seeing relatives again, of renewing friendships, of encountering smiling faces. I wake up in the morning to see palm trees swaying in the wind, and ancient stones gilded by the sun. During the day I shake a thousand hands.

"In the confusion of my arrival, I had a surprise. Said, my old Said, came to welcome me with the classical wish: 'Ahlan oua sah'lan.' It is not surprising that he has remained in our family's service for twenty-five years. It was something else that surprised me. I had known him to be quarrelsome, vindictive, brutal, a women-chaser, and an incorrigible drinker. Today he is gentle, patient, and humble. He does not raise his voice. His gestures are sober and deliberate. A certain indefinable and inexpressible serenity emanates from him.

"To clear up the mystery, I questioned Said a few days later, as our long friendship allowed. He answered, 'God willed it. God willed that.' That was all. He didn't explain. Said knows my religion and sincerely respects it, but he will not let me penetrate into his inner life.

"Not content with such an evasive explanation, I went to his home one morning. He lives in the heart of the Arab Quarter, in one of those houses with whitewashed walls. He lives with his wife Zohra and the abandoned child he adopted. It is a strange oasis of peace and order, contrasting with the hubbub of the neighborhood. It was eight o'clock. I went to Said's room but, contrary to the laws of Oriental hospitality, he made no effort to welcome me. He was at prayer. I later discovered that Said did not limit himself to the five daily ritual prayers, but spent considerable time in prayer or meditation besides. Was this his secret, the explanation of his transformation?

"While I waited for Said, I was told that he begins to pray every day at dawn, and then goes out to work until mid-afternoon. Once back home, he resumes his prayer. During this time the whole household keeps silence. Only afterward does the coming and going of visitors begin. Said is known in his neighborhood, and his neighbors come to ask his advice. He settles the myriad daily quarrels that are submitted to his arbitration. He does not allow anyone to publicly give him the title of 'sheikh' to which he has a right. However, he is unanimously respected, and is surrounded with more attentions than a venerable marabout. He is always ready to chat, and his words are filled with a wisdom and gentleness that amaze anyone who knew the Said of earlier days. At night he prays again at length before going to sleep. He spends not less than five hours with his God during the course of a day.

"When Said had finished praying he came to me, invited me into a tiny drawing room, and offered me the traditional cup of coffee. In a word, he received me with all the refinements of exquisite Oriental hospitality.

"After leaving him, I returned homeward slowly. It was my turn to meditate. . . ."

* * *

Do you understand why I wanted you to read this letter? It clearly shows that Said's prayer life is the source of the transformation of his character and of his moral life, and not the reverse. My friend made no mistake about it. I grant you that self-mastery is necessary to anyone who wants to progress in mental prayer. But prayer is even more necessary in order to arrive at self-mastery. Indeed, I greatly fear that if you wait until you have acquired self-mastery before you devote yourself to mental prayer, you may never succeed in either.

Anyway, the expression "self-mastery," that you use, seems open to debate. A Christian has better things to do than to aspire to self-mastery. He should rather be striving to let God have mastery over him. Consider Said. Do you think that if he had merely attained self-mastery, he would have had this magnetic influence on those around him? Through his transformed and pacified personality, the presence of Another within him shone forth and attracted.

Seek God, surrender your spirit to the growing dominion of his love, and you will soon discover that order and peace will take root within you. St. Augustine vigorously and clearly expresses this great law of the spiritual life:

* * *

It is fitting that the inferior be subject to the superior. He who wants to dominate what is inferior to himself, must submit to what is superior to himself. Your own submission is to God, and the flesh (and all its inclinations) must submit to you. What could be more just? What could be more beautiful? You are subject to what is greater than you. If you break the first law: "You owe submission to God," then the second law will never be carried out: "The flesh owes submission to you."

* * *

There is a privileged means for achieving the submission to God of our whole being. It is mental prayer. Said bears witness to it, as have countless Christians over the centuries.

93. *"You will see my back"* (Ex 33:23)

Your letter brought to mind a woman of lowly estate whom I encountered over thirty years ago. As a young priest, I was then living with a colleague who had rented me a room near the Basilica of Montmartre.

A woman from the neighborhood came to do the housework, and I sometimes chatted with her while she was sweeping my room. She seemed very old to me. Today I would have quite a different idea of her age! She was tiny, nimble, discreet as a shadow, and seemed always to be apologizing for existing.

She was certainly very virtuous—I should say very holy. But to realize it, one had to take a close look at her eyes. They were the only chink into her interior world, from which shone an intense and pure light.

She would pray for hours at the Basilica on her knees, her eyes fixed on the monstrance. It was whispered about that she gave half of her meager salary to others poorer than herself.

I had to give you this brief description, so you could grasp the significance of the dialogue I am going to relate to you. It is at once elliptic and very rich in spiritual meaning.

* * *

One day, when I was preparing to preach a retreat, I said to her, "Pray that I may be able to speak well to them about God." And she answered, almost inadvertently, "Oh! Above all, don't talk about God!" Then, embarrassed by what she had just said, she apologized: "I'm really stupid. I don't know why I said that to you." And I couldn't get her to say another word.

In any event, I was greatly intrigued by her curious little statement, spoken with so much conviction. It was probably from that moment that I took an interest in her spiritual life.

Something else she said, after hearing a sermon, enabled me to grasp her thinking a little better. She confided: "I was so happy. The preacher said that we cannot understand God." "But don't you have a great desire to know God?" "Yes, but not to understand him. It's always when I think that we can't understand anything about God, that I feel as if I'm surrounded by a very calm light."

* * *

Was I wrong in surmising that you would find the answer to your questions in these words spoken by a very simple woman?

Unless we stop trying to know God by our own means, we shall never really come close to him. We must not only go beyond the knowledge of the senses, but also beyond rational knowledge. Many prayerful souls are stymied in their search for God, because they are not willing to mortify their imagination and sensibility. They limit themselves to intellectual notions of God, not realizing that God will not let us grasp him through our concepts, any more than the ocean allows itself to be caught in the fisherman's nets.

This humble woman knew that beautiful ideas can at best carry us only a short distance on the road to God, but that when we cling to them they prevent us from penetrating the mystery of God. She was saying in her own way what Bossuet said in more eloquent, if not more insightful, terms concerning "God's sublime incomprehensibility":

* * *

"The further we advance in our knowledge of God, the more we see, as it were, that we know nothing worthy of him; and rising above all that we have ever thought about God or that we can ever think of God throughout eternity, we praise him in his incomprehensible truth and are lost in this praise."

* * *

We must give up, once and for all the hope of knowing God here below as he really is. Then God can infuse into the center of our soul a knowledge of himself that is both the luminous certitude of his existence and presence, as well as the complete ignorance of what he is in himself. It amounts to seeing God's back, the way Moses did. *"When my glory passes I will set you in the hollow of the rock and will cover you with my hand until I have passed by. Then I will remove my hand, so that you may see my back; but my face is not to be seen"* (Ex 33:22-23).

While we remain on earth, we cannot contemplate God's face. St. Thomas Aquinas has written a deeply penetrating commentary on this subject:

* * *

"When we have reached the limit of our knowledge, we know God as unknown. And our intellect attains in a very perfect manner to the knowledge of God, at the precise moment it knows that the divine essence exceeds everything it can grasp in the present state of life."

* * *

One of the best proofs of the presence and action within us of the gift of wisdom, the most sublime gift of the Holy Spirit, is our love for the incomprehensibility of God. We rejoice in hearing others speak of it, and dread to hear statements that claim to reveal God to us. Likewise, we feel a need during prayer to allow ourselves to be engulfed in the abyss of divine incomprehensibility, the way a pearl fisher dives into translucid waters.

Before we reach this stage, however, we must spend a long time seeking the discursive presence of God by meditating on his word, and by contemplating his attributes as they are mirrored in his creatures. It would be presumptuous to want to advance at a faster pace than God's grace does.

Yearn with all your might to know God. Seek him. Abandon yourself totally to him so that he may lead you into this realm, infinitely beyond anything our human faculties of knowledge can explore. Meanwhile, remain very poor and small, and he will reveal himself to be very great indeed. Love his darkness, and he will welcome you into his light.

* * *

On one occasion Jesus spoke thus: "Father, Lord of heaven and earth, to you I offer praise; for what you have hidden from the learned and the clever you have revealed to the merest children. Father, it is true. You have graciously willed it so" (Mt 11:25-26).

94. The mental prayer of a woman of the people

I f this woman of the people heard me speak of her *method of mental prayer*, she would smile that serene and timid smile that was characteristic of her. And she would be right. I could even imagine a nuance of gentle irony in her smile.

How poor we are, for all our wealth of technology and methods! This woman didn't have a method of prayer, any more than she had a method of smiling.

* * *

She came to seven o'clock Mass almost every morning. When I distributed Holy Communion, she stood out from the others by the quality of her recollection. Indeed, it is impossible to define this quality. She seemed to experience something so delightful, deep within her, that a mysterious radiance emanated from within and made her face flush. I was also impressed by her recollection when she knelt in the chapel, head held high and hands joined.

One day as we chatted, I took the liberty of asking her how she prayed. At first she seemed surprised. But since for her a priest's question was something to be taken seriously, she reflected for a moment and answered: "At the start of my mental prayer I think of the fact that God has his own ideas, and wants something from this moment that I have come to spend with him. Then I want what he wants, and seek no further. That's my whole prayer."

* * *

Well, I can tell you that this is a very authentic, sublime and perfect kind of mental prayer. If you reflect on the modest words you have just read, you will find that they contain the highest virtues in a very exceptional degree: faith, abnegation, surrender and love. There is faith in the living God who is fully attentive to his child, and who will certainly make this mental prayer serve the intentions of his glory. Abnegation: there is no self-seeking or self-oriented desire here, not even the most purified desire. Adherence to God's will is certainly sufficiently present in her prayer. For her, it is a surrender to whatever the Lord will do, an unconditional acceptance of everything he will ask. And finally love is present. It is a love close to adoration, and consists in yielding all the room within us to the God whom we love.

On another occasion, she confided to me how she had arrived at this form of mental prayer. I'm sorry that I can't reproduce the exact words she used, because hers was the simple, down-to-earth speech of a woman of the people. But here is the substance of what she said:

* * *

"I went through a very painful phase. During mental prayer my desire to know and love God became so strong and so compelling, that it left me completely shattered and exhausted. This desire didn't seem right to me. I thought I ought to repress it, because it might involve self-seeking. I knew I should come before the Lord empty of any desires. That didn't bring me any peace, either. Then I tried to think of great intentions that would be pleasing to my God: the conversion of unbelievers, the reunion of the Churches, an end to war. But I was never quite sure that the intention I had chosen was exactly the one God had in mind. Weeks passed. I still felt that my mental prayer failed to meet the Lord's expectations.

"Finally, one day an idea came to me that was so simple I was surprised I hadn't thought of it sooner. Since I was never sure of acting according to God's preference, why not be content to want with all my strength whatever God wanted deep within me, communing with all my will to God's will? Or better still, why not let the divine will envelop me totally? Then I would be sure of not making a mistake, of not disregarding God's wishes with respect to others and myself. Then I could be sure of offering him exactly the prayer that he was expecting of me. This time I was at peace deep inside of me. Since then, whenever I don't find inner peace, it is a sign that I have allowed myself to be distracted from God's will. And so I turn back to it at once."

95. *Beacons along the road*

M adam, I should like to comply with your request that I retrace the spiritual development of your late husband, but that is not easy. How and by what stages, did he achieve the resplendent spiritual life that so impressed those around him? It's true that I was the witness to, and the confidant of, his spiritual efforts over many years. But the most important things happened within him, at a depth to which I had no access. Even so, I shall try to retrace the principal stages in his life of prayer, as I thought I discerned them.

When I met your husband almost twelve years ago, he was a man of profound faith, as you know better than I. He almost always reacted to the events of life as a believer. When one of his children was sick; when he had to make an important business decision; when you had your serious accident—his first reaction was to turn to God. You remember his great faith in the Fatherhood of God, which he expressed in Christ's own words: *"Ask and you shall receive. Seek, and you will find. Knock, and it will be opened to you"* (Mt 7:7).

One day, I sensed that he had entered a new spiritual phase. During a conversation with him, it became clear to me that for several months his prayer had been undergoing a transformation. He was no longer petitioning God for temporal goods. He was seeking the riches of the Kingdom, and he was doing it with great insistence! When I pointed out to him that it is perfectly legitimate to pray to God for our temporal needs, he did not argue with me. But, in a tone that touched me deeply, he reminded me of Christ's words:

* * *

"It is not for you to be in search of what you are to eat or drink. Stop worrying. The unbelievers of this world are always running after these things. Your Father knows that you need such things. Seek out instead his kingship over you, and the rest will follow in turn" (Lk 12:29-31).

* * *

Your husband was filled with a very keen desire for the grace which he was experiencing more and more. It was a grace that led him to correct his faults, and inspired him to a more profound prayer. It was a grace of peace and joy which, through him, touched the souls of those who came to him for counsel. It was at this time, as you must certainly remember, that he devoted himself with so much love to helping a young delinquent boy.

A few years later, I came to realize that this stage had also been exceeded. One day, when we were speaking of mental prayer, he quoted the following words of a mystic: "What a great difference there is between the person who goes to the feast for the feast's sake, and the one who goes to encounter the Beloved!" Very often during the following months, in his conversations and letters, certain verses from the Psalms would recur that revealed his state of soul:

* * *

"O God, you are my God whom I seek;
   for you my flesh pines and my soul thirsts
     like the earth, parched, lifeless and
        without water" (Ps 63:2)
"Athirst is my soul for God, the living God.
   When shall I go and behold the face of God?" (Ps 42:3)
"I stretch out my hands to you;
   my soul thirsts for you like parched land" (Ps 143:6).

* * *

When I talked with him, it was clear that he no longer aspired to the riches of this world or even, in a certain sense, to those of the Kingdom. He now yearned not for God's gifts, but for the gift of God himself.

Years passed, and this yearning continued to consume him. He was eager to read the great spiritual authors, and to meet persons who would speak to him of his God. It was as if he kept hoping to discover a secret: the means of encountering this God who had captivated him, so as to never again be separated from him.

There was something extraordinarily poignant in this need for God, at once impatient and peaceful, that welled up from the depths of his being. It manifested itself in his conversations with me, and certainly must have found expression in his mental prayer through heartrending cries. I believe I can safely say that your husband had attained to authentic evangelical detachment, not through scorn for the good things of the earth, but thanks to the fascination he had for an incomparably more desirable Good.

Then there was a time when I was baffled. I kept wondering whether his fervor was declining. I no longer perceived the throbbing of his heart consumed by a fever for God. Even so, I was not worried, because peace and joy—I was about to say, the Holy Spirit—poured from him. I had proof of this in his growing influence on others. It was at this period of his life that he prepared the Jewish professor for baptism, the one whom you welcomed so graciously into your home.

I continued to misidentify the work of grace within your husband, until the day he unknowingly gave me the key to it by speaking about a state "beyond desire." I questioned him about it. Here is his answer almost word-for-word:

* * *

"It's true that for years my entire spiritual life consisted in an insatiable desire for God. Then one day, it was as if all desire was dead. I was very frightened. I was convinced that I had lost God. The sentiment of intense life, fed by the desire to encounter the Lord and lose myself in him, was superseded by a void, a spiritual languor. I didn't know if I still had faith. I was certain that I no longer loved God, since I could not discern the slightest desire for him within me. You were not there to help me understand God's will. I felt as though I had emerged from a long-lived illusion. I was both calm and desolated—the way one speaks of a desolate land.

"I saw the light when I remembered, with a certain nostalgia, the prayer which had so often escaped my lips during the preceding years: 'Lord, I hunger and thirst for you.' For the first time, I understood that this prayer was not poor enough: 'I hunger . . . I thirst . . .' The 'I' was still too much in the foreground. It was far too much alive, when it should have been crucified.

"One after the other, I had renounced the good of this world, and then the goods of the Kingdom. Now I had to renounce even the desire for God. I mean, that I must no longer desire union with God for my sake, but for God's. This union must no longer be a desire emanating from me, but a desire emanating from God within me."

***

That day, we talked for a long time about this new stage in his life of mental prayer.

Several months later, when you informed me of his accidental death, I was reminded of a passage from Emile Dermenghem's *Vie des saints musulmans* (Lives of the Muslim Saints), that he had quoted to me with intense joy during our last conversation:

"A voice cried out to me, 'O Aboû Yazîd, what do you desire?' I answered, 'I desire to desire nothing because I am the desired and You are the one who desires.' "

96. It's you

A Muslim student came to see me. He had read one of the issues of *Cahier sur l'oraison*, and wanted to meet me. At the end of our conversation he told me, with exquisite courtesy, that he wanted to leave a Muslim legend with me in remembrance of his visit, and as a sign of his gratitude. And he added, "I'm sure you will like it very much."

Actually, I like this legend so much, that my entire letter to you today will consist in acquainting you with it.

***

One night a lover, filled with audacity and the spirit of conquest, knocked at the door of his beloved. She asked, "Who's there?" He answered, "It's I." She refused to open and said harshly, "Go away!"

With wild rage, the young man went off swearing that he would forget her, and that in fact he had already forgotten her. He traveled over the wide expanse of the world. But he could not forget. And love brought him back irresistibly to his beloved's door. There was the same dialogue as before. However, this time, when she sent him away, she added a mysterious little sentence: "You have still not said the only word that would permit me to open to you."

Indignant, baffled and crushed, the young man went off again. This time, he didn't go to seek forgetfulness in journeys to distant lands. He went down into solitary gorges, to spend long hours in meditation. Gradually, his anger and passion gave way to wisdom. His love gained in depth what it had lost in violence. After many years, it led our lover back again, this time timid, humble, and more ardent than ever, towards his beloved. He knocked discreetly at her door. "Who is there?" In a low tone of voice he answered, "It's YOU." And immediately the door was thrown open.

* * *

My Muslim visitor made no comments on his legend. Indeed, what need was there for that? It is as clear as a running stream. To engage in mental prayer is to knock at the door behind which the great life of God is ablaze, resplendent with light, love and joy. When the person who knocks is stripped of self, and has surrendered all the room in his soul to the Lord, he can say in all truth: "It's You." Then the door opens to the long-desired union with God.

97. God's rest

You are perplexed because you feel inclined to rest during mental prayer whereas, until now, you had the sense of engaging in intense activity of mind and heart. You wonder whether it is a temptation to indifference.

Do you not perhaps have, along with so many of our contemporaries, a rather low esteem of repose, reserving your enthusiasm for action? Of course, distinctions must be made. There are many kinds of repose. But to suspect all repose *a priori* is a serious error. If certain kinds of rest are nothing but sloth and indolence, there are others—and they deserve respect—addressed to nurturing and renewing strength for the sake of more effective action.

There are nobler types of rest, as well. Read the Epistle to the Hebrews (Heb 4, passim). It gives us "good news," the promise of entering into God's rest. It is reserved for the people of God, and therefore offered to each of its members. The author of the Epistle concludes: *"Let us strive to enter into that rest"* (Heb 4:11).

The expression "God's rest" is a very ancient one. In the Bible, it is used to designate the Promised Land. To enter into this land is to accede to God's rest. But the Promised Land is only an image, and a very imperfect one, of God's true rest to which we are invited. And that is Heaven. Like the Promised Land, Heaven must be laboriously conquered. Does this mean that we must renounce seeking God's rest, before entering the Homeland? No. On the road, we are provided with divine stopping places: hours and places of rest. Didn't Jesus Christ say: *"Come to me, all you who are weary and find life burdensome, and I will refresh you. . . . learn from me, for I am gentle and humble of heart. Your souls will find rest"* (Mt 11:28-29)?

We can, indeed we must, seek God's rest. We must strive to enter into it, as the Epistle to the Hebrews exhorts us to do. But let us delve even more deeply into this Biblical notion of God's rest. The expression "God's rest" must not be understood only as the rest that God offers us. It is also the rest that God himself enjoys. Let me explain.

It is true that we think more readily of God's intense activity, than of his rest. We are less surprised to hear Christ say, *"My Father is at work until now, and I am at work as well"* (Jn 5:17), than we are to read these words: *"God's rest"* (Heb 4:10). Reflection on love can help us to interpret these words correctly.

At first sight, because love is a reaching out, a desire, it seems contrary to rest. But reaching out and desire are not the whole of love. They are impelled toward a goal: communion. In communion, love becomes repose. This repose is not the exhaustion of the reaching out and the desire, but their unfolding in calm, joyous ecstasy.

This is true even within the life of the Triune God. The Father and the Son love each other with an infinite love. They reach out to one another with immense, irrepressible mutual desire, are united, and rest *"in the unity of the Holy Spirit."* That is why the Holy Spirit has been called "Repose" by the Church Fathers. Indeed, this Repose of the Father and the Son is not the extinction of their love. In it, this love finds consummation and fulfillment in infinite, eternal exultation.

If all love aspires to rest, and finds fulfillment in it, how can we attain to God's spiritual rest here on earth? I'd like to give you some insight into the answer.

The love relationship between the Christian and Christ is, like all love, first of all a matter of reaching out and desire. It tends towards its perfect fulfillment, repose in closeness with the beloved. The Book of Revelation says so in concrete terms: *"Here I stand, knocking at the door. If anyone hears me calling and opens the door, I will enter his house and have supper with him, and he with me"* (Rv 3:20). In John's Gospel, Christ expresses the same truth in less concrete but stronger and terser terms: *"you in me, and I in you"* (Jn 14:20). So we see that already here on earth, Jesus Christ wants to give us a foretaste of God's rest, by uniting us to himself.

Anyone who faithfully practices mental prayer cannot fail to experience this, at least at times. As a proof of this, the spiritual writers speak to us of a form of mental prayer called "prayer of quietude," prayer of rest. Listen to what one of these writers has to say:

* * *

"When the soul presents itself for mental prayer, even if it comes with the intention of concentrating on some specific subject, it at once finds itself—without knowing how—recollected within itself, with a sweet sense of Our Lord's presence. It is true that this sentiment is not very distinct. But its sweetness persuades the soul that the One it loves is near and comes to express God's love, and it must therefore think only of enjoying the happiness offered to it" (Father Joseph Picot de Clorivière, S.J.).*

* * *

And in the measure that the Christian succeeds in praying without

* French Jesuit, 1735-1820.

ceasing, in accordance with Christ's command, he can very well live without ever leaving God's rest, even amid a life of feverish activity.

Let us go farther still. This Christ toward whom we are reaching out, and whom we desire, is not content to welcome us into his close friendship. He wants to sweep us up into the arms of the Father, in an incoercible surge of love.

And so the soul that is malleable in God's hands is introduced into the intimacy, the communion of love, between the Father and the Son. This communion is the Holy Spirit. For Tradition has given these names to the Holy Spirit: Repose, Feast, Jubilation and eternal Acclamation of the love of the Father and of the Son.

You may well answer: "You are making me dizzy. I'm a long way off from that kind of holiness." I agree, but isn't the repose that you experience in your mental prayer already a first step on the road to "God's Rest"?

Other Books On Prayer
From Alba House

GOD IS A SEA
By: David Walker
"The seed of God is in us. Given an intelligent and hard working farmer it will thrive and grow up to God, whose seed it is, and accordingly its fruit will be God-nature. Pear seeds grow into pear trees, nut seeds into nut trees, and God seed into God." Eckhart

This book contains reflections on the cultivation of the God seed within human existence. They explore the nature of the divine life to which it gives birth, the means that can be used to facilitate its growth, and its ultimate expression in prayer.

$4.95, paper

MEDITATIONS ON THE SAND
By: Alessandro Pronzato
Written after a pilgrimage to the tomb of Charles de Foucauld in the Sahara, this series of meditations concentrates on the paradoxical nature of prayer. The reader is shown how to create an interior desert of solitude, silence and prayer amidst the rush of everyday life.

$5.95, paper

CALLED TO INTIMACY
Living The Indwelling Presence
By: George A. Maloney, S.J.
This noted spiritual writer shows how the indwelling Trinity calls us to ecstasy through the power of divine love. By loving self-emptying and self-abandonment we can allow the inner light of God to fill us and radiate to others. Based on the best of the Western and Eastern Christian mystical traditions, this book will appeal to a wide audience.

$5.95, paper